# QUOTABLE
## CRYPTOGRAMS

# QUOTABLE
# CRYPTOGRAMS

· 500 FAMOUS QUOTES TO DECIPHER ·

## TERRY STICKELS
· and ·
## SAM BELLOTTO JR.

**Random House
Puzzles & Games**

New York    Toronto    London    Sydney    Auckland

# CONTENTS

# INTRODUCTION

**L**OOKING for a new puzzle that's as challenging as it is fun? If you've never experienced the world of codes, ciphers, and secret writings, then welcome to the world of cryptograms. Cryptograms remain one of the most popular forms of puzzles in the world today. They can be solved with a myriad of languages, fonts, pictures, and numbers, and you can take your pick from easy to mind-numbingly difficult. Plus, they increase your mental flexibility and keep your mind limber and young.

Cryptography is the study of creating and solving codes, ciphers, and secret messages, from the Greek "kryptos" meaning hidden and "graphein" meaning writing. There are many types of cryptograms, and methods for solving them vary widely.

People have been solving cryptograms for fun for over 600 years. But records as far back as the fifth century BC reveal that the Spartan army used coded messages to carry information during war campaigns. During World War II, breaking Japan's PURPLE machine cryptogram enabled the US Navy to be victorious at Midland Island. Today cryptography is used in information security, access control, and authentication. ATM cards, computer passwords, and virtually all aspects of the digital world have some relation to cryptography.

Do you think you have what it takes to crack these codes? This book contains over 500 cryptograms—from puzzles for beginners to puzzles for the gurus of code breaking. If you've never solved a cryptogram before, don't worry. We teach you step-by-step how to tackle each type, and if you get stuck, there is a hints section for the more difficult puzzles. If you are looking for more challenging puzzles, those are mixed in as well.

Each cryptogram is a famous quote from a famous person, so you'll not only have fun solving the puzzles, but reading the answers as well!

My good friend and colleague Sam Bellotto Jr. and I hope you enjoy solving these puzzles as much as we did putting them together. Comments? Questions? Go to www.terrystickels.com and send us an email. We'd love to hear from you.

*Terry Stickels*

# HOW TO SOLVE THE CRYPTOGRAMS IN THIS BOOK

"AND HE PUZZLED AND PUZZLED 'TILL HIS PUZZLER WAS SORE." —*Dr. Seuss*

*Call them what you will. Cryptograms. Ciphers. Encoded messages. There are more than 500 of them in this book, and they cover several types of cryptograms. In this section we'll go over each type and show you how to solve each one. Many are substitution ciphers, but we've also included some Rail Fence, Quagmire, and Playfair ciphers (plus a dozen or so "specialty" cryptograms to keep you on your toes).*

## SUBSTITUTION CIPHERS

Substitution ciphers are the most popular type of cryptograms. There are many types of substitution ciphers, but what they all have in common is that the cryptogram retains the character count and word spacing of the original text, but different letters are substituted. To solve this type of

cipher, make the best guesses you can about certain words or letters, replace them, and by trial and error see if your guesses make sense. In this
book you will find three types of substitution ciphers:

# • • CAESAR CIPHER • •

This method is named after Julius Caesar, who used it to communicate with
his generals. In this type of cipher, the natural order of the alphabet is maintained, but the positions are shifted three spaces. An A becomes a D, B becomes an E, and so on. Here's an example:

```
THIS IS A CAESAR CIPHER
```
*becomes*
```
WKLV LV D FDHVDU FLSKHU
```

Please keep in mind that when solving the cryptograms in this book that
ciphers can be built in this way by shifting the position as much or as little
as possible. In one puzzle, A=B, B=C, and C=D, while in another, A=K, B=L, and
C=M. These cryptograms are the easiest to solve. Guess one letter correctly
and you can build the entire shifted alphabet. Similarly, if several attempts
at deciphering with a shift pattern don't make sense, the puzzle must be a
different type of cryptogram.

# • • RANDOM LETTER
# SUBSTITUTION CIPHER • •

The typical and most widely-known kind of cryptogram involves a random
substitution of one letter in the plaintext alphabet with another letter of the
ciphertext alphabet. No letter stands for itself and there is a one-to-one substitution between the alphabets. For example, all of the Bs may be replaced
with Ms, and the Fs with Ys. For example, the phrase

```
CRYPTOGRAMS ARE FUN PUZZLES TO SOLVE
```

*becomes*

```
MIZUGARIFXH FID CNQ UNSSBDH GA HABLD
```

To begin cracking this code, a reasonable guess for FID would be ARE.

## •• *QUIPTICS CIPHER* ••

This is a type of cryptogram developed by our very own Sam Bellotto Jr. The Quiptics cryptogram adds the actual inter-word spaces into the encryption mix, which means that a space within the cryptogram may not actually be a space at all. A space could represent the letter R. By the same token, the letter G may represent a space. For example,

```
CRYPTOGRAMS ARE FUN PUZZLES TO SOLVE
```

*becomes*

```
UPJBRNMPZ IYZPDYSXEYBXQQADIYRNYINAGD
```

In this puzzle, the letter Y represents the space and the space represents M. Quiptics cryptograms are intended for advanced solvers, and there will be hints available in the "hints" section to help solve each one.

## RAIL FENCE CIPHERS

The Rail Fence Cipher is different from substitution ciphers in that all of the letters in the plaintext appear in the encrypted text unchanged but scrambled. There is no substitution involved. The key to the scrambling is why it is called a Rail Fence Cipher. In this cipher, the message is divided into columns of alternating rows, resembling a rail fence and the number of rails can vary. (In this book, they vary from 2-4 rails.) First we'll show you the steps to encoding a 2-rail cipher:

We'll start with the phrase:

QUIPTICS IS THE GREATEST

1. Count the number of letters in the plaintext. Here there are 21.
2. To make this a two-rail cipher, it must be divisible by 2, so add random letters at the end. These are called "nulls" and have little impact on understanding the decoded message. This message needs one null: QUIPTICS IS THE GREATESTX
3. Divide the message into 2 sections alternating the letters and eliminating spaces. The pattern for a 2-rail cipher is a zig-zag:

Q I T C I T E R A E T
U P I S S H G E T S X

4. Combine the two lines into a single long string, by putting the second line after the first. The encoded message reads QITCITERAETUPISSHGETSX
5. Break the message into chunks of letters equal to the number of rails, which becomes the "key," as a default. QI TC IT ER AE TU PI SS HG ET SX indicates this is a two-rail cipher. QTIE TUIS BXIC TEVP SHSW indicates a four-rail cipher.

Now working backwards, let's try to decode the following:

TRI TUI HFO TSN HPM KNA ESO EPR

We see from the groupings of letters that this is a 3-rail cipher.

Remove all spaces, format on a single line, and count the length. TRITUIHFOTSNHPMKNAESOEPR gives us a 24-character rail. (The length of each rail will always equal the length of the single line.)

We will need 3 rails, then, which plotted out, using periods as place markers, looks like this:

. . . . . . . . . . . . . . . . . . . . . . . .
. . . . . . . . . . . . . . . . . . . . . . . .
. . . . . . . . . . . . . . . . . . . . . . . .

Now mark the w-shaped pattern, for our purposes using an x.

```
X...X...X...X...X...X...
.X.X.X.X.X.X.X.X.X.X.X.X
..X...X...X...X...X...X.
```

Finally, replace all the x's with letters from the cryptogram going from left to right. Do the first rail, then the second rail, then the third rail, and so on.

```
T...R...I...T...U...I...
.H.F.O.T.S.N.H.P.M.K.N.A
..E...S...O...E...P...R.
```

Reading up-down-up following the conventional w-shaped pattern, the cryptogram is decoded as THEFROSTISONTHEPUMPKINRA. Easy enough to determine the spacing. And the last two letters are "null" and therefore ignored. The answer is:

THE FROST IS ON THE PUMPKIN

# PLAYFAIR CIPHERS

Playfair ciphers are complex ciphers generated from an arbitrary 5×5 matrix using all the letters of the alphabet except one. For the purposes of this book, that letter will always be the letter Q. Any Qs that appear in the plaintext are automatically converted to K. Thus, the word EQUAL will be spelled EKUAL. The word QUAKER will be spelled KUAKER.

The Key Table is made by filling in the matrix cells, left to right, top to bottom, with all 25 letters of the alphabet (Q is not used). Start with the keyphrase, dropping any duplicate letters. Then add the unused letters of the alphabet, in order.

Here's an example Key Table using CONUNDRUM as the keyphrase:

```
C O N U D
R M A B E
G F H I J
K L P S T
V W X Y Z
```

To encrypt a message, break the message into groups of 2 letters known as digraphs. Encrypt the new pair and continue. For example,

CRYPTOGRAM *becomes* CR YP TO GR AM

If the two letters are the same (or only one letter is left), add an "X" after the first letter. For example,

BOTTLE *becomes* BO TX TL EX

Now encode using the key table. Each pair of letters has a corresponding pair in the key table.

Let's use BO as an example. The B and O on the key table form a rectangle, and the opposite corners of the rectangle are MU. So MU is the coding of BO. RY on this key table would be BV. AT would be EP. The coding will always be the "opposite corners" of the rectangle formed by the original two letters.

If the letters appear on the same row of the table, replace them with the letters to their immediate right respectively (wrapping around to the left side of the row if a letter in the original pair was on the far right side of the row).

For example, on this key table CO is encrypted as ON. HI as IJ. BE is ER. ST is TK.

If the letters appear on the same column of the table, replace them with the letters immediately below respectively (wrapping around to the top of the column if a letter in the original pair is at the bottom of the column).

For example, on this key table CR is encrypted as RG. HP as PX. SY as YU. LW as WO.

Following these rules, here is how CRYPTOGRAM is encrypted:

```
CR YP TO GR AM
RG XS LD KG BA
```

Finally, spaces are eliminated with the finished puzzle looking like a solid block of text. CRYPTOGRAM encoded would be RGXSLDKGBA.

Even experienced Playfair solvers could not crack a puzzle without help. With each Playfair cryptogram, a few letters or a short word is given to start you off. The hint phrase is in lower case next to the puzzle number, e.g.:

23 (PLAY) THISISTHECLUE

For all other levels of solvers, even knowing a few letters will still leave you thoroughly stumped (although you may want to try). Beginning or intermediate solvers are encouraged to turn to the "Hints" section of this book which includes the keyphrases upon which the puzzles have been encoded. Use the provided keyphrases to construct the Key Table. Break the cryptogram into digraphs and decode the puzzle using the same rules as the encoding process.

For instance, given the keyphrase CONUNDRUM, you can quickly construct the key table as explained previously:

```
C O N U D
R M A B E
F G H I J
K L P S T
V W X Y Z
```

Given the coded phrase RFXSLDFMBA, apply the same rules for decrypting as explained above for encrypting. The only difference is that two letters appearing on the same column get shifted up, and two letters appearing on the same row get shifted left.

```
RF XS LD FM BA
```

RF is decrypted as CR. XS is decrypted as YP. LD is decrypted as TO. FM is decrypted as GR. BA is decrypted as AM. The answer is CR YP TO GR AM. Or CRYPTOGRAM.

# QUAGMIRE CIPHERS

The Quagmire cipher is devilishly complex, based upon a number of cryptographic elements. Basically, a Quagmire cipher is made from a ciphertext table that consists of stacked alphabet rows below a key row:

*the key row*

A B C D E F G H I J K L M N O P Q R S T U V W X Y Z

*the alphabet rows*

A B C D E F G H I J K L M N O P Q R S T U V W X Y Z
A B C D E F G H I J K L M N O P Q R S T U V W X Y Z
A B C D E F G H I J K L M N O P Q R S T U V W X Y Z
A B C D E F G H I J K L M N O P Q R S T U V W X Y Z
A B C D E F G H I J K L M N O P Q R S T U V W X Y Z
A B C D E F G H I J K L M N O P Q R S T U V W X Y Z

The top row is the plaintext alphabet. Beneath is the ciphertext table. Shown above before applying any keywords. Quagmires can have up to three different keywords.

The top plaintext row is formed using a keyword much the same way the Playfair matrix is formed. Begin with the keyphrase, dropping any duplicate letters. Then the unused letters of the alphabet, in order. Using TERRY STICKELS as the keyphrase, the key row comes out:

T E R Y S I C K L A B D F G H I M N O P Q U V W X Z

The rows in the ciphertext table are then formed using the same keyphrase as the key row, or another keyphrase altogether.

Let's use CRYPTOGRAM as the ciphertext table keyphrase. The entire ciphertext table would look thus:

*the key row*

T E R Y S I C K L A B D F G H I M N O P Q U V W X Z

*the alphabet rows*

```
C R Y P T O G A M B D E F H I J K L N Q S U V W X Z
C R Y P T O G A M B D E F H I J K L N Q S U V W X Z
C R Y P T O G A M B D E F H I J K L N Q S U V W X Z
C R Y P T O G A M B D E F H I J K L N Q S U V W X Z
C R Y P T O G A M B D E F H I J K L N Q S U V W X Z
C R Y P T O G A M B D E F H I J K L N Q S U V W X Z
```

However, Quagmires all use an indicator ("period") key. The indicator key establishes the "period"—the number of rows in the table—and the letter with which each alphabet row begins. If the indicator key is SAMUEL, 6 letters long, it would direct a "period" of 6 rows thus:

*the key row*

```
T E R Y S I C K L A B D F G H I M N O P Q U V W X Z
```

*the alphabet rows*

```
S T U V W X Y Z A B C D E F G H I J K L M N O P Q R
A B C D E F G H I J K L M N O P Q R S T U V W X Y Z
M N O P Q R S T U V W X Y Z A B C D E F G H I J K L
U V W X Y Z A B C D E F G H I J K L M N O P Q R S T
E F G H I J K L M N O P Q R S T U V W X Y Z A B C D
L M N O P Q R S T U V W X Y Z A B C D E F G H I J K
```

Combine the indicator key SAMUEL with the ciphertext table key CRYPTOGRAM and we get the actual table to use for encoding the plaintext:

*the key row*

```
T E R Y S I C K L A B D F G H J M N O P Q U V W X Z
```

*the alphabet rows*

```
S U V W X Z C R Y P T O G A M B D E F H I J K L N Q
A M B D E F H I J K L N Q S U V W X Z C R Y P T O G
M B D E F H I J K L N Q S U V W X Z C R Y P T O G A
U V W X Z C R Y P T O G A M B D E F H I J K L N Q S
E F H I J K L N Q S U V W X Z C R Y P T O G A M B D
L N Q S U V W X Z C R Y P T O G A M B D E F H I J K
```

The indicator key does not always have to appear down the first column. It can be any of the 26 columns, adjusting the alphabet rows accordingly. This is the same ciphertext table with the indicator key in column 10:

*the key row*

```
T E R Y S I C K L A B D F G H I M N O P Q U V W X Z
```

*the alphabet rows*

```
E F H I J K L N Q S U V W X Z C R Y P T O G A M B D
X Z C R Y P T O G A M B D E F H I J K L N Q S U V W
Z C R Y P T O G A M B D E F H I J K L N Q S U V W X
F H I J K L N Q S U V W X Z C R Y P T O G A M B D E
Y P T O G A M B D E F H I J K L N Q S U V W X Z C R
M B D E F H I J K L N Q S U V W X Z C R Y P T O G A
```

As is evident, with the period key running down column 10, the first row starts with S in column 10 and wraps after D. The second row starts with A in column 10 and wraps after W. And so on.

Encoding is relatively simple. Locate each plaintext letter on the keyed plaintext row (top) and replace it with the corresponding letter of a ciphertext table row, depending upon period order. The first letter of the plaintext is replaced by a letter from the first ciphertext table row, the second letter from the second row, the third letter from the third row, and so on. If the period consists of six rows, after the sixth letter, cycle back to the first row.

Quagmires are conventionally broken up into five-character units. So based on the table above, the phrase

```
CRYPTOGRAMS ARE FUN PUZZLES TO SOLVE
```

*becomes*

```
LCYOY CXCMY GLHZE AQRGW XSPFE KPTDT F
```

A **Quagmire I** cipher uses a keyed plaintext row run against a straight cipher table.

A **Quagmire II** cipher uses an unkeyed plaintext row alphabet run against a keyed cipher table.

A **Quagmire III** cipher uses both a keyed plaintext row and a keyed cipher table sharing the same keyword.

 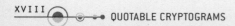

A **Quagmire IV** cipher uses a uniquely different key for the plaintext row, the cipher table, and the period key.

For the Quagmire cryptograms in this book, a few letters or a word are revealed in the puzzle itself to start off those who relish solving quagmire puzzles from scratch. The hint is in lower case to the right of the puzzle number, e.g.:

23 (QUAG) THISISTHEHINT

Everyone else is encouraged to refer to the "Hints" section from which they can build the ciphertext table.

*Key:* CHRISTMAS
*Cipher Key:* STOCKING
*Indicator:* SANTA /13

In this Hint example, the plaintext keyphrase is CHRISTMAS, the cipher table keyphrase is STOCKING, the indicator key is SANTA, and it appears in column number 13. Constructing the ciphertext table yields:

*the key row*

C H R I S T M A B D E F G J K L N O P Q U V W X Y Z

*the alphabet rows*

J L M P Q R U V W X Y Z **S** T O C K I N G A B D E F H
W X Y Z S T O C K I N G **A** B D E F H J L M P Q R U V
U V W X Y Z S T O C K I **N** G A B D E F H J L M P Q R
L M P Q R U V W X Y Z S **T** O C K I N G A B D E F H J
W X Y Z S T O C K I N G **A** B D E F H J L M P Q R U V

If you know the Key words to a Quagmire cipher, you must build the ciphertext table prior to decoding. Top-level solvers can figure out the Key words themselves and then build the ciphertext table. To decrypt JYQGTIAWWO, locate J in the first row and read the equivalent letter from the key row at top. C. Locate Y in the second row. R. Q in the third row. Y. And so on. After row 6, begin again in the first row. The answer is quickly revealed to be CRYPTOGRAM.

# SUMMARY

Most of the cryptograms included in this book are standard cryptograms. You can identify them because the word lengths and spacing are maintained. The Quiptics-style cryptograms also maintain word lengths and spaces. However, as the spaces have been substituted for a letter and a letter may actually be a space, the size of the words may seem quite long.

Rail Fence ciphers are comprised of equal-length letter groupings according to number of rails used to encode the puzzle. Rail Fence ciphers are displayed in letter groups of 2, 3, or 4.

Playfair ciphers are presented as solid blocks of text with no spaces and even rows all the same length, except the bottom row. Playfair ciphers are also indentified by (Play) appearing next to the puzzle number.

Quagmire ciphers are presented as groups of 5 letters with nine groups per row, except for the bottom row. Quagmire ciphers are also indentified by (Quag) appearing next to the puzzle number.

Hints to assist in solving the Playfair, quagmire, and quiptics ciphers can be found in the HINTS section of the book. One word is also revealed with each Playfair and quagmire cipher to get you started if you choose to solve these puzzles from scratch. Solutions to all of the puzzles can be found in the back of the book.

Good luck!

# ANIMALS

"ANIMALS ARE SUCH AGREEABLE FRIENDS,
THEY ASK NO QUESTIONS, THEY PASS NO
CRITICISMS." —*George Eliot*

## 1.1

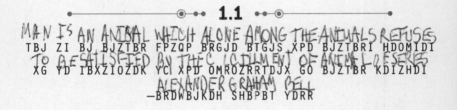

MAN IS AN ANIMAL WHICH ALONE AMONG THE ANIMALS REFUSES
TO BE SATISFIED BY THE (FILMENT OF ANIMAL DESIRES

TBJ ZI BJ BJZTBR FPZQP BRGJD BTGJS XPD BJZTBRI HDOMIDI
XG YD IBXZIOZDK YCI XPD OMROZRRTDJX GO BJZTBR KDIZHDI

ALEXANDER GRAHAM BELL

—BRDWBJKDH SHBPBT YDRR

## 1.2

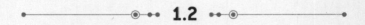

DSDBR TZBJVJA VJ QHBVYQ Q AQLDKKD OQWDC GM VU WJZOC

VU TGCU ZGUBGJ UPD HQCUDCU KVZJ ZB VU OVKK ID WVKKDN

DSDBR TZBJVJA VJ QHBVYQ Q KVZJ OQWDC GM VU WJZOC VU

TGCU BGJ HQCUDB UPQJ UPD CKZODCU AQLDKKD ZB VU OVKK

CUQBSD VU NZDCJU TQUUDB OPDUPDB RZG QBD Q KVZJ ZB Q

AQLDKKD OPDJ UPD CGJ YZTDC GM RZGN IDUUDB ID BGJJVJA

—QJZJ

## 1.3

(Quag) retrieverswhen

VNHRW XFSSB WYDNQ MZPYL GWECZ XZQJC INCPZ JPDCV NFMKN

TDYWR UCYWX SQUOD QPQUL UACIQ MNINS KQPUO BXBJW DGRZX

PWTHC WEJOZ TCDYH WEHNW XYJOF FQXZJ KMLUY ZVOBL KZMZX

CUALI WBBBE YQRYH KXLPN MFNDA DAWMY DFPNM WLVVF ZXCLS

OFSPP IVNGE WFIWA DCUFZ VDMMN KKNLY IUOBK NJZNK KC

## 1.4

(Quag) thecodfishlays

HRBLR ZHOYF NNGBH MIDQK WMVIO JMJMD FMQKA INWRJ XTZJR

QFCVB MYQHO NMRIM ZCSVV YSVCB HQLMV ICWEU RNNBB MRORX

GZZNY REGML ZWFNK ILZOK VBBGF XVCVB MFEIY TIRBZ CCRCX

XMCPN VRZZV GJWMR DRWKW GWQYN KZDAD STCMD ZVHDG CDAYJ

TDWZW TRBB

## 1.5

IY UH ND GC NC UT RP TI GH ED GI CI SN OR OK TN GV

FD OL TO HL AT RT FO TI KO SA TO NT YU TN TR EO BS

UT IY UP CE AD IE IO NY WP IP SO EJ

## 1.6

TOS DEU SLU NNO LLA IUN FUL ADD OOJ SRA HDG ASL OBE

SCE SUI PLI GAU TIS EEO SGC TBT AHS RQE TYR GET EOD

WTH SAE TUB REH EMN CFN LMP TVF AYM AEN DGH GNI MHE

## 1.7

IAUR ATPI AIOA FWNC RUDB DAHT OLTL VSNT IJYO
YUTO EOOS BEJS UATE OITE LTLN OTYG RURL RHEE

## 1.8

(Play) understand

CLEDBDLSFKRNDXZFOBMARBCNPJSPABLKCKNEDLWSZFOAAVEGAE
EOOFLBNLHISOFLEGEOWDMPLPHPLCAERBAZSADMHLOZJRIEANGL
HNEKGARBRAPJFLSRFLLSCKBRPHTUIPNPHIIAKABPGRHEEKFLCB
IEHFGMFOHPRAAL

## 1.9

(Play) savechildren

IFTCGVOFMHOFLDBWSMCIIVDLHNWTXDDWOMJLFIJPILJLGHBNBO
GZNTGVKXWSATXDTMIBLDCTTSJMATOFXTOFWEAOVLBLDMAJSAJM
CAOMROFINLLBENANBGIHLJNBIWIFTCGVOFMHOFDBWAGNMVMOBO
AZ

## 1.10

(Play) expressionof

ARJBITSLPRLBEWMUZXTHAFEUJOHPBWMUPIAWRWTRIJXGTEHPBL
DLPRPBIREFBLRTPMBDPDADRUCTTWSABOURMEMGMDUCDAHLBTBK
SWTHHPNLPTFNTBPOTWTBUPONESBZETVEPELXRIDCEFEMCSCTPB
ISEF

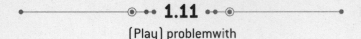

## 1.11

(Play) problemwith

SJOUDRLFBUOGSJLCUTNPSJJYSJDZKOSYSJRZRZCLUTLTBCRWEG
RISJOCBHCLOZKRSJBDSJDZURDCPBSJRDCANYBUSEEBDBOSCTIC
WISCRTPDCR

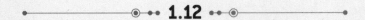

## 1.12

ZN M ZRMVSRP ND HMUOYMORI ZSRPR VNGRI
M ZBGR TSRU ZSR TNPHK BI JYZ M QHMVR ND GMUL
TNPKI MUK GMU MQQRMPI M GRPR ZMHXBUO MUBGMH
UNZ GYVS GNPR TNUKRPDYH ZSMU M QMPPNZ
—ENIRQS VNUPMK

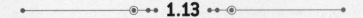

## 1.13

JSD ODBKJS GMH YROEK BSE MJOKDK BOD MBVVH RK YDNBWKD
XMDH BOD SJX XOHRSI XJ RTVODKK JXMDO YROEK BSE MJOKDK
—EBQD NBOSDIRD

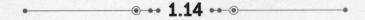

## 1.14

WJOWRQ PZEZECZP W LWM JGGAQ SGOX GX EWX W SGT
JGGAQ VK MG EWX CVM W KFT OFJJ JGGA EWX PFTBM FX MBZ
ZRZ WXS QZZ BFQ ZYVWJ
—OFXQMGX LBVPLBFJJ

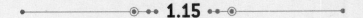

## 1.15

DBP PXPOBWQD BWE W DBRTM EMRQ W BPWK LJXX CL
RYCVI WQK WE PYPVICQP HBC BWE EPPQ W TRVTJE OWVWKP MQCHE
OVCTPPKE UPED UI SVWEORQS DBP DWRX CL RDE JVPKPTPEECV
—WKXWR P EDPYPQECQ

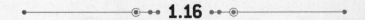

## 1.16

NRXDIKXNKN KDUU ON KPLK KPD HLNKDNK LIXFLU MI DLYKP
QXKP L KMG NGDDC MH MID POICYDC KQDIKZ HDDK GDY NDRMIC
XN L RMQ KPLK PLN ADDI CYMGGDC MOK MH L PDUXRMGKDY
—CLJD ALYYZ

## 1.17

KAUQB LAU NVHPZB KAB HNQQPTB ZPDPV GUCB QKZFWKFZBQ UI
VPCUQNFZQ QAUFMV ZBHBHGBZ KANK RBMMXIPQA QKPMM BCRUX
KABPZ TBZX QBWFZB BWUMUDPWNM CPWAB
—GBNF QABPM

## 1.18

FTQ DQMEAZ U XAHQ YK PAS EA YGOT UE NQOMGEQ ITQZ
U OAYQ TAYQ TQE FTQ AZXK AZQ UZ FTQ IADXP ITA FDQMFE
YQ XUWQ UY FTQ NQMFXQE
—NUXX YMTQD

# •• *EASY LIVING* ••

Standard substitution cryptograms don't necessarily have to use the alphabet. This example uses nautical flags. Each unique flag represents one letter of the alphabet.

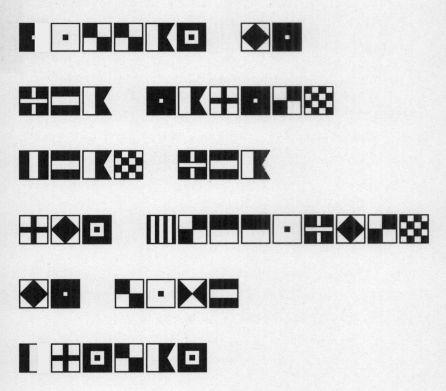

# ART & LITERATURE

"BOOKS ARE HUMANITY IN PRINT."
—*Barbara W. Tuchman*

 **2.1**

RLTJILYLNV LR NMD ELAFI FYMLDUDTDAN FENDB CAD MFR
JIFVDP F UFRN XSFANLNV CE ACNDR FAP TCBD ACNDR LN LR
RLTJILYLNV NMFN DTDBHDR FR NMD YBCKALAH BDKFBP CE FBN
—YMCJLA

 **2.2**

DLQZQ SZQ PSRB USBI AY WZQSTXRC S LQSZD
IDAZXQI UQZQ YFNN AY LQSZDI WZATQR WB NAJQ WFD
ULSD ZQSNNB WZATQ S LQSZD USI DSTXRC SUSB
XDI GZQSP —ULSDQJQZ DLSD GZQSP PXCLD WQ
—VQSZN WFOT

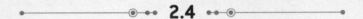

## 2.3

HCTK JCXV RCYJBEGUTH UT QWCQGW
ALC XEBK AJUKW UBKWJPUWAUBI QWCQGW ALC
XEBK KEGV SCJ QWCQGW ALC XEBK JWEZ
—SJEBV OEQQE

## 2.4

V NZMDJPN RMDOZM DN IJO OJ WZ XJIAJPIYZY
RDOC V NJGZHI RMDOZM V NZMDJPN RMDOZM HVT WZ
V CVRF JM V WPUUVMY JM ZQZI V KJKDIEVT WPO V
NJGZHI RMDOZM DN VGRVTN V WGJJYT JRG
—ZMIZNO CZHDIBRVT

## 2.5

SP WI RECLKXN GYEVN OFOB WOOD K GYWKX YX
DRO CDBOOD GRY VYYUON VSUO DRO GYWOX SX RSC ZKSXDSXQC
RO GYEVN PKVV YFOB SX K NOKN PKSXD
—WBC ZKLVY ZSMKCCY

## 2.6

JHJOILMJ YTX CTRJMC NYTC WX OTOJ WX CYJ QLSOTBJ CL
ELRRLN CYTC CTRJMC CL CYJ VTOF KRTQJ NYJOJ WC RJTVX
—JOWQT ULMB

## 2.7

RP QJDNI Z URHXIN QJD GJUI QJDN OJRBI Z VZUIVZGG

KGZQIN GJUIU ERU ZNL Z CNRYIN XIYU LJNI SHJCGIMXI ZHM

RP EIU XJJM YEI JGMIN EI XIYU YEI VIYYIN EI CNRYIU

—LRBSIQ UKRGGZHI

## 2.8

DBJL W CKGJA SQ WP JY JKL SQ MJFJYUG

SQ TEKWLX JYC PGKGYWLX CGOSWC SQ LKSEMFWYN SK

CGTKGPPWYN PEMHGUL AJLLGK J PSSLBWYN UJFAWYN

WYQFEGYUG SY LBG AWYC KJLBGK FWRG J NSSC JKAUBJWK

DBWUB TKSOWCGP KGFJZJLWSY QKSA TBXPWUJF QJLWNEG

—BGYKW AJLWPPG

## 2.9

F UHVE VDE AVMTHE NJU WFMHX VL DFSRL VMJDS

LRH QHVYR AUFLFDS QVE QMVDT OHUXH VDE XHVUYRFDS

HDEMHXXMZ NJU XJWHJDH AJDEHUNPM ARJ AJPME

XLHK JPL JN LRH EVUTDHXX VDE YRVDSH WZ MFNH FL DHOHU

YUJXXHE WZ WFDE LRVL LRVL KHUXJD YJPME QH WH

—VDDV GPFDEMHD

## 2.10

COZN G PASHRK UL NOY NKGRZN ZNK NKGZ GTJ ZNK IUXVYKY
UL HKKY XKBURBOTM RGFORE XUATJ NOY SOTJ PGSKY HUTJ
YZXURRKJ ULL OT ZNK JOXKIZOUT UL ZNK ZGRR MXKE
HAORJOTM CNUYK AVVKX YZUXKEY YNUCKJ ZNKSYKRBKY GHUBK
ZNK ZXKKY OZ CGY ZNXKK ZNOXZE UTRE ZCU SUXK NUAXY ZU
MU HKLUXK NOY TKDZ JXOTQ
—OGT LRKSOTM

## 2.11

QSLQFGLC GQ BCJGAGMSQ PYGL GQ PCDPCQFGLE UGLB ZPYACQ
SQ SN QLMU GQ CVFGJYPYRGLE RFCPC GQ LM QSAF RFGLE YQ
ZYB UCYRFCP MLJW BGDDCPCLR IGLBQ MD EMMB UCYRFCP
—HMFL PSQIGL

## 2.12

PDA HEXANPU KB PDA LNAOO EO W XHAOOEJC
SDAJ SA WNA EJYHEJAZ PK SNEPA WCWEJOP KPDANO
WJZ W YWHWIEPU SDAJ SA BEJZ KQNOAHRAO KRANXKNJA
XU PDA IQHPEPQZA KB KQN WOOWEHWJPO
—OWIQAH FKDJOKJ

## 2.13

PDA KHZAN SA CNKS PDA CNAWPAN XAYKIAO KQN
SKJZAN WP DKS IQYD ECJKNWJYA KJA YWJ YKJPWEJ
SEPDKQP XQNOPEJC KJAO YHKPDAO
—IWNG PSWEJ

## 2.14

JUT B TIBNF UIBU UIF PDMZ UIJOH B NBO
DBO EP GPS FJHIU IPVST B EBZ JT XPSL IF DBOU
FBU GPS FJHIU IPVST IF DBOU ESJOL GPS
FJHIU IPVST IF DBOU NBLF MPWF GPS FJHIU IPVST UIF
POMZ UIJOH B NBO DBO EP GPS FJHIU IPVST JT XPSL
—XJMMJBN GBVMLOFS

## 2.15

ZYNP HSPY SP HLD DVPENSTYR YPLC ESP DPL
L WTEEWP RTCW HSZ SLO QLWWPY TYEZ ESP HLEPC
HLWVPO MJ HTES OCTAATYR NWZESPD WPHTD
NLCCZWW EZCP L NZCYPC QCZX L ATPNP ZQ MWZEETYR ALAPC
LYO DLTO XLJ T ZQQPC JZF ESTD EZ MWZE JZF FA
—XLCETY RLCOYPC

## 2.16

ICERWCXKRXQHHMXXUQOROLETMVXRKCCNRAMZVMMXR
IROLERLIARWCXKRXQHHMXXUQORHJMW HLORMIZ
IMMVXRKCCNRAMZVMMXR IRHJMW HLORMIZ IMMV IZREJ
HJRLKROMLXKRXQZZMXKXRKJLKRKJM VRXHJCCO IZRJLARLRA
VMHKRDMLV IZRCIRKJM VRXQHHMXXR IRKJM VRHJCXMIRU
MOARKJMIRJCERHCWMRWCXKRXQHHMXXUQORLQKJCVXRKCCNRAMZVMMX
RICKR IRMIZO XJRO KMVLKQVMRDQKR IRXCWMRE AMOTRA
UUMVMIKRU MOARYCJIRERHLWSDMOO

## 2.17

DUJDWHUMYMKHMKHUDEUPQWHKUIOUETHUVZQDMU
HJJKUXQMEQKCUDKUQUMH
HKKQZCUDMSZHNDHMEUDMUJDBDMSUDEKUJYYWDMSUQEUJDXHUETZYIS
TUETHUPZYMSUHMNUYXUQUEHJHK YOHUPTD
TUDKUPTQEUDUNYUQMNUETQEUHMQVJHKUCYIUEYUJQISTUQEUJDXHKU
ZHQJDEDHKU
—NZUKHIKK

## 2.18

(Quag) keepyourmouthshut

RJBHR YVGVN KXOPO ELSWD LNLCI OSVUM SJURO DZZGY VGKRM
VSSZO PUHFZ DUQZL AOSVM KSRVO OFDQY YDXJB SESCO ESIYC
MKEAH ZWDFF DUFZL FBACQ IRNFQ OVWGY MCZKS TUBZR KSTNI
GCBWE AFSCY RLNES LMDOG QUHOM SOBIV KSTVF YSYAX KRFJU
ESRPN AFCJJ YHLYR

## 2.19

### (Quag) underthepretense

```
FJQBP YAIVL WXMEF NYHYU DJBZO URKGL RXLJQ XMTTN NFOTD
JYXJK HNPYM HOJVG JVDLL FQPXU ISMCK IVXYW KYSWO NDGOB
GJBSO ZDUVJ VJDLD OOXPA TIBIO GVJBY DIHNY HYTJR RYVTT
QBCNK DJXHP KRNHC IPRBB PDWZH SVREB BKXYT JHSHR XZQLA
          IIEQS UYJHT S
```

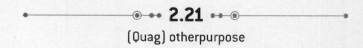

## 2.20

### (Quag) fumbleruleisa

```
NDOGR QYEOZ ZRISI FNWNJ KEBDK BQZFC NQRJY WWRJE IWANL
RFSWQ TJBBG UKMMC KRQOI ROSLT BDWOI MJAGR WKZDO QMMZS
WDCLM DXXAL GJIRO ERBTB MELSH RJBHC WWJPU BXBMZ FBJTH
PFCKT WVVDH RJLHD KRNLZ RNQQY ZWANT RFQEX RWZLN IVPYJ
ORJEH RQLKE EUARL MYSMN LRNSH EKIIC WQHLY CKRKH SCYIR
          JYHYO AFLLP GGZXD FOQVX AY
```

## 2.21

### (Quag) otherpurpose

```
FGDFZ NDMDY XMOUM NJENB BCAQR WSOXW SZEZZ UBYMH LQWQF
HZLZG KBGMY RJOXS BTTND QBWKZ XCDMD YXMOU MNYNH XBYZU
HLEZR ZSQFN ANZPP ZLPRE SSYNS WGNAX OMYWI WELUD DVBLE
          BTQHQ MGRVI ABYCM Y
```

## 2.22

### (Quag) ringlardner

```
EZCDE HXYHK TIGEE MQKUG FDYXI MTYEM HQXCU OLTIB VLAFC
WPIOF XAZDA BPHOV MYTAK CDAGT DHKVM AYNYX IJGHT ZCSPG
XNZES IGKOU OQBTM SKESD DPNMI KTLYA FQDTH HYXIV TLHAH
XZBSA ASTDR SZJMC KPHYE MHTDQ YRZWY BQFCA RPDHA IYLQU
SZXMK XBRMN YLFTE MO
```

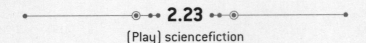

## 2.23

### (Play) sciencefiction

```
YMKBMDFOJBRUTFJRTPFCPNULEPHKFDAKIHPRRPSODTURVCHSFR
VCPBDFOBJGESLYFSGURUHDPNBFJACOVOFSMTODSTSPEROTIHKB
MTBSGKZDOBYMFRFDRCGKTOYSDZUHOTBVOSUPBOOBTOXBIHWPDF
SFDFIWUHJMSFLBHURUTFVOPNGKERKFUHGNJNUHYCPKLZFDCGTL
IPBU
```

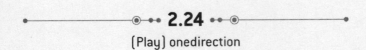

## 2.24

### (Play) onedirection

```
XGDUIWLONRIADMKUDPGLKPEADCHPUDCLPXDMBLCTDPGLKPEADC
HPUDFLDJSJLDFELTPNODXGBIGSCEDYSJGODZSJDWWEDCMDCJMU
RFLALCIOMDRFSJDWWEDCSYPNPIDZFNDFLY
```

AT SH DS RO AA TE PE SI SL TR CR TE EC IN OH SE SN
LT TT EO LH LV SN ML WL RI TE EI EF MN OX RS HM EF
OE OD HR AT OS FI PR OA IY OH WR DE IE IA YO EL

EYP ISU WEO OAO EDT SIN TIL DCN HTA SUF SLE OEA NWS
CEP TPE CRI VRC MUS OIP TPN RTR TBC MSF FLT OEI NAD
TRL IPO ETD CIE EET OTT EAI NLN TTT OAT ADE TRS MYA
SGA DOI UTE LNT EUI ZRR ZSN LIL WSH EOL NUO ISE EEI
BEN EER SEN LIO NOI IER NTS ERO NMD IHL EII AER

MHYGHZT HR VHJQ P RUHSQKR BQN PGGPYCQS QOQK RZ VHFCGVD
UQKCPUR NWG RGHVV PGGPYCQS GZ VHMQ PG PVV MZWK YZKTQKR
ZMGQT GCQ PGGPYCXQTG HR RYPKYQVD UQKYQUGHNVQ
—OHKFHTHP BZZVM

OBK VAZ OT YU SGTE KTOMSGY GTJ VAFFRKY ZNGZ OZ CORR
QKKV ZNK VXULKYYLXY HAYE LUX IKTZAXOKY GXMAOTM UBKX
CNGZ O SKGTZ GTJ ZNGZY ZNK UTRE CGE UL OTYAXOTM UTKY
OSSUXZGROZE
—PGSKY PUEIK

## 2.29

L NWLDDTN TD DZXPESTYR ESLE PGPCJMZOJ

HLYED EZ SLGP CPLO LYO YZMZOJ HLYED EZ CPLO

—XLCV EHLTY

## 2.30

O CUARJ KYVKIOGRRE ROQK ZU XKIUAXZ ZNK SAYK UL VUKZXE

CNU XGT ULL COZN ZNK SGORSGT LUAX EKGXY GMU GTJ JXUVY

SK UTRE G YIXOHHRKJ VUYZIGXJ LXUS ZOSK ZU ZOSK

—PUNT AVJOQK

## •• NOTE OF CAUTION ••

This cryptogram uses different symbols. For example, the "smiley face" icon represents the letter K.

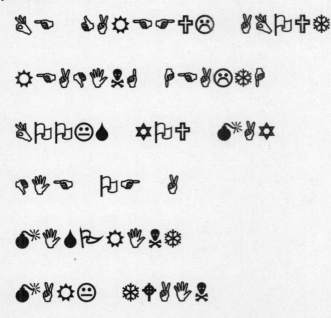

# BUSINESS

"IT IS DIFFICULT, BUT NOT IMPOSSIBLE,
TO CONDUCT STRICTLY HONEST BUSINESS"
—*Mahatma Gandhi*

## 3.1

PO EPVE DC FB EPO FWDXDFX IFXOJ YDKK LF OUOAJEPDXN

IVJ YOKK QO CTCWOHEOL FB LFDXN OUOAJEPDXN BFA IFXOJ

—QOXRVIDX BAVXMKDX

## 3.2

VTVJ CJ UFQL AVQLJCQIZ ZCJVU IU VJRCJVVECJR IDPFA

SCSAVVJ XVEQVJA PS PJVU SCJIJQCIZ UFQQVUU CU OFV AP PJVU

AVQLJCQIZ WJPHZVORV IJO IDPFA VCRLAG SCTV XVEQVJA CU

OFV AP UWCZZ CJ LFBIJ VJRCJVVECJR AP XVEUFJIZCAG IJO

ALV IDCZCAG AP ZVIO XVPXZV

—OIZV QIEJVRCV

### 3.3

ODY CVSNTUYSOTI MFGSBGMIYR PDGBD XJAYFS ODY DTSNIGSX
JC MJROTXY ROTUMR TSN JC UGIIGJSR JC NJIITFR TFY
YHTBOIQ ODY RTUY ODYQ TFY ODY BJUUJS ITP JC ZVRGSYRR
TSN ODY PDJIY MFTBOGBY JC BJUUYFBY GR CJVSNYN JS ODYU
—M N TFUJVF

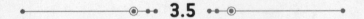

### 3.4

CFUVGHUU VU DVJH IVD VQ XIGO
LVQ XVOB KGEOBVGZ CFO CFUVGHUU
—M ZAKBKL

### 3.5

SPO QOBS OCOTYSNDO NB SPO EJO IPE PKB BOJBO
OJEYLP SE MNTZ LEEA ROJ SE AE IPKS PO IKJSB AEJO KJA
BOXV—HOBSHKNJS SE ZOOM VHER ROAAXNJL INSP SPOR
IPNXO SPOG AE NS
—SPOEAEHO HEEBODOXS

### 3.6

C VHTS RTHZ SBN RNL SH GDQCNGG ODS SBN RNL
SH YXCUDEN CG SELCTP SH IUNXGN NKNELOHVL
—OCUU QHGOL

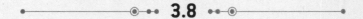

## 3.7

U RDJPMAJJ HYUH IUNAJ MGHYPME RDH
IGMAL PJ U OGGV NPMW GZ RDJPMAJJ

—YAMVL ZGVW

## 3.8

RW BRFPUZ NBVSBIU DW ZDTV YGKBY
SDCB WVDC UMBIUZ NBVSBIU DW GKK ZDTV RUBCY
QTYU SGVVZ UPDYB UMBIUZ NBVSBIU

—PBIVZ HRYYRIFBV

## 3.9

AIG BI YEOZJU NELZ YEL IKKIFYGZOYOLU SIRL
VQIZJ OPL EVB KLFOIBU OZ RA QODL NELZ OPL EVB
V MGZBQL ID OBLVU SIRL VQIZJ VZB OPL EVB QIZJ
BFA UKLQQU OD O JLY VZ OBLV ZLWY NLLC OQQ
BI UIRLYEOZJ OD ZIY O NIZY BI V BVRZ YEOZJ

—NVFFLZ MGDDLYY

## 3.10

QBRW ABGY RLVCHHQ NRGYBAOWG CWO
QBRW IWOCYOGY GBRWNO BE KOCWLMLI

—SMKK ICYOG

### 3.11

DFU SCN BRGHRGXDCRYL XGU LQTTUYZI DXJCYN
YRDCBU RM DFU VUS XYT DFUCG GUXBDCRYL FXKU SUUY
LZRV UKUY DFU BREHQDUG CYTQLDGI MXCZUT DR LUU
DFU CEHRGDXYBU RM DFU CYDUGYUD SQD DFXDL YRD LXICYN
EQBF ZUDL MXBU CD DFU BREHQDUG CYTQLDGI MXCZUT
DR LUU DFXD DFU BUYDQGI VRQZT UYT

—TRQNZXL XTXEL

### 3.12

FADFVDHMPHV BAZM VDVMCGVI BAZM HOAZCOHI PDS
BAZM FPNGHPW HOV XGIV YPD NZHI PWW OGI VCCI GD
ADV KPIEVH PDS XPHFOVI HOV KPIEVH

—PDSMVX FPMDVCGV

### 3.13

Q SPYU UVQYO ILBMG VBKL BYF CAGQYLGG CLQYH SLSANUQCML
QI ZPJ GLWBJBUQPY PZ NBMPJQLG BYS NPJWPJBUQPYG

—JBMWV YBSLJ

### 3.14

WDSYI STD JL STZ VPTJ PZGDT ODPOYD OSNHZ MDSXZNVXYYL
PH QSHESI PT CTNZD CPHWDTVXY OPDZTL N YNRD JSRNHF
WDSYI OTDVDTSMYL MNF WDSYI

—WPHSYW ZTXJO

## 3.15

IRQ AMKSV CMV SIA PD NPGBVCKCKPR GIX WV YPGVCKGVY MIHQ
DPH CMV KRQKZKQTIS KC KY WVYC DPH CMV HINV WVNITYV KC
VRYTHVY CMV YTHZKZIS PD CMV DKCCVYC KR VZVFX
QVBIHCGVRC
—IRQHVA NIHRVUKV

## 3.16

UE BSX WYZURXZZPHR GVYAM ZBVC BHANURL AUNX H JVPCYBXK
CKURBVYB VK H CHLX EKVP BSX JVKCVKHBX HRRYHA KXCVKB
VBSXK CXVCAX GVYAM ZBVC BSURNURL SX SHM H JHZS
KXLUZBXK EVK H SXHKB
—SXRKF NUZZURLXK

## 3.17

PG
QVJXOXFSHEPZHTQHGQOAVXTQGHPOHJBQHOAXQFAQHIWHPVVJOJXFSH
JBQHBNEPFHXFJQCCXSQFAQHCIFSHQFINSBHJIHSQJHEIFQZHWVIEHX
JHOJQRBQFHTNJCQVHCQPAIAD

## 3.18

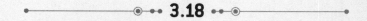

RSPBFLZI LTY LGTRTYIYTSP KZTGBLTYLRIFLMHFLJHIPYTYF
YZBQBLT L SRBYZTPELMBFSPCLTYIPCLYZIYLT LJHIGTYFLLUQIPX
GGSFCLKQTEZY

## 3.19

NGHSPLANSTLQHCKRBSTGHCLPLYHSJYLQYSNLSAMEHYMHSEASNGHSPL
YHUSTGHCLPLYHSNGHSMLCTLCXNHSQLCBWSEASALSARKKRAHWSQENGS
ENSNGXNSXBPLANSXYULYHSQLCJEYDSEYSARMGSXYSHYZECLYPHYNSQ
EBBS HSWCEZHYSPXWSQENGEYSXSTHCELWSLKSQHHJASEKSULRSWLR
NSNGEASULRSYHHWSLYBUSZEAENSYHQSULCJSMENUSXYWSL
AHCZHSNGHSHKKHMNSLKSNGHSTCLOEPENUSLKSQXBBSANCHHNSLYSXS
PXILCSRC XYSTLTRBXNELY

—WXZEWSDHCCLBW

## 3.20

VHIWHD ILXSI EIAZHAXZHI EIWHIXIAZEOZXCCHZIRDI
EILZR HIAZEOZXCDIXTBI EID NBSIOZHX IAZEOZXCDI VX IE
VHZIAHEAJHIVXGHILZR HTIRTICSIYXDHIRILHT I EI
VHIOXZWXOHIYXTDIX I VHIYECAN HZIDYRHTYHIYHT
HZIXTBIRIKRDVHBIEN IJRD RTODIEKI VHRZIEAHZX
RTOIDSD HCI

—WRJJIOX HD

## 3.21

(Quag) the waterfront

QJJVQ PZAGX VDVBO MKJPP GPXOX NZONU RLOPO TFYFV PUOCI
XPIEI QVMSP YMLEJ TJHNP HQJIX GSQJE BNUZZ MVRYP YMLEJ
TJHNP HPAIR ASKJF VBIRK HFOYA CGRGO MZDTL BQDOO NMBJF
VLKBJ FGOMZ BQVPL APZLE XYGOP LNZQT RTSZO IVNUZ YHBRX
TCPBK LTLUL LYVP

(Quag) boughtbymen

```
ECZHO  KOPCD  EBNVY  DAZPZ  NMISE  CPJGX  SNBFE  NIFHL  VJVST
JGXAA  GOVYO  JGFJX  VAIWS  UNTRG  AZAAF  TCWZV  BQATN  SHIUC
CLHXV  XXLTU  ATZQB  DJRER  CDEZW  BHDOC  CNMIQ  ALSMS  KXXQW
IGCYN  UIAOZ  CAHIV  OSTGA  QGZIJ  GXKRR  XCBZB  DIKHW  VYHOR
GAAZQ  DVFBE  VXDNI  QRGGK  KSRQV  FBSMN  UHNOA  TZADE  VXDNI
QLXZV  FVMDR  WHICY  WYWDR  OZVPD  KQUVG  JSUAY  WFCUE  YKD
```

## 3.23

```
TMHM  UOBE  NTLR  GLOE  YRBY  FDHR  ETEY  AORN  MOUV  RIGE
AELE  YNHL  SHLL  AASF  ETOA  SNKE  YEAR  SOLN  NEOY  HYEY
HARI  SSVT  IEEA  WEAN  PTEI  HTWJ  HENF  INIC  WSTT  LEHS
                     TSDH  GHON
```

## 3.24

(Play) thecompetition

```
TOSEPJBTJZIPTREYPHBTUKGEAGRBLUMBYLPLUKDESEHLELBTWA
BASUBRTAGSYLNWNDMBXRHDTATIBAAGPGUORSBEBELARJXRAKTA
MTBETAGSDBMWMFTOTMSMEFSGSETIENYNMLSEJZAO
```

## 3.25

```
II  DT  AH  RA  YO  OT  AA  UI  ES  AB  IG  LN  RT  EC  UL  NI  CM
EE  TO  EN  TR  LY  OE  ON  LE  EF  NI  RT  EE  ST  PR  RY  BS  NS
MN  EN  BA  DA  HR  RE  AD  NO  PT  NC  MS  AU  AL  TM  JH  CE  SY
```

## 3.26

```
IA TM KS MO TM SI AS MT OS OE TH RV NE AG TN EK HE
WR VS TD YN LE NM DU OI AW OF ES OH RH SD AC DE HO
OY IB RH DO AE OE PI IT CS UP IN TM ET EE EU TR EI
WE TR EE EI IE BA AI NA ED TX NG HO FR TS AE IA VN
            ET CN LG DL ET
```

## 3.27

```
IY UA TO NR AE OR UC SR TD UL YU FI UE AE HM SA SN
FO WN TI CE SY US CE SA EO BE OR AL RR TT OA WT OI
```

## 3.28

```
OT TN IG ED RG OT FH WY OO ST EE FS EM FH IP RO NL
FE PE EI VI TE SL EI SM ZN WA TE CN CO PI HA WL OU
SA DN LA ES OU OT EA TB OT HS LE TE OT ER ES NE IP
   OL BL EE NH ME VS TA AI GH TH YA AC ML SS MA TN
```

## 3.29

```
II UF RU AE EA TU MN BS NS EE UI EF RH TH YR WR HN
SL TE FR HT HY HN TE AE OT ML OM OB ST SN OT NT WC
NB YA YU IE SX CT VS OW AT EA EO TA DE LH MO WA TE
         TI KH YR WR HA CL FR ET
```

## 3.30

```
IWE  GAO  OEI  OUR  NRK  AOA  YMI  EDL  ERU  EVT  BRM  ORG  RRT
SEL  NUH  HTE  PEF  HNT  ODN  TNE  SAD  UBN  IGN  MNT  RSS  EFR
FHY  IIE  IVT  EEO  LBA  EOU  INE  OEO  ORW  ONN  HNY  ODI  LOT
     PLT  ANO  DTO  AND  EYT  OTD  BEH  WDR  LOF  TRM  IEF
```

## 3.31

```
GSW  CDMBWHAMGJ  IR  MQQMDIMA  STA  SMHWF  RMRGWWD  YIKWD  GI
AKWQQ  UME  KTDCHW  TQQ  FTJ  AI  GSTG  HWAWTHZSWHA  ZTD  RMDF
ICG  YSTG  KTVWA  UME  KTDCHW  AKWQQ  AI  LTF  JIC  VDIY  YSI  M
RWWQ  AIHHJ  RIH  GSW  YIKTD  YSI  TUUQMWF  RIH  GSMA  CIL  TDF
                    EIG  GCHDWF  FIYD
                    —OTJ  QWDI
```

## 3.32

(Quag) itisnosecret

```
IRSHM  MOKZV  UBQYF  REVTX  AIWUY  JDZED  STIWB  LBQPB  XJKQS
TXSBL  IEVBE  EIMDS  XBFUM  DPOPW  MDPVB  ZZXBH  GCAPK  YFVXH
ZYYXD  NPQED  HFNYZ  FMDWE  ZBJNT  UJMAX  BYUOP  PHYII  KCVFI
SPANB  JHHKN  DDTBI  IWCGU  EEZSA  XKQJF  YLZKQ  LEXGD  FMDUM
```

This cryptogram uses the famous "Dancing Men" symbolic alphabet introduced by Conan Doyle in his classic Sherlock Holmes adventure of the same name. There are no spaces. Figures holding flags are used to determine the last letter of each word.

# ENTERTAINMENT

"FILM IS ONE OF THE THREE UNIVERSAL
LANGUAGES." —*Frank Capra*

## 4.1

H AUXGGSO KSNHSDHPB HP ARPUR JNRVA FISP H
FRA AHT WXUISZ UXXQ WS UX ASS IHW HP R OSGRZUWSPU
AUXZS RPO IS RAQSO EXZ WL RVUXBZRGI
—AIHZNSL USWGNS

## 4.2

VZ KOIKFII J GBTJL VZ HT JIIZETG VZ QETJV ZWTB IZRTIM
IJHZB VZ HT PFWTR J XDJRXT VZ XBTJVT FQ VDT LTJV JRG
UZVJVZTQ ZK IFKT VDT LZRTM FQ VDT PBJWM
—HTVVT GJWFQ

## 4.3

N LXIR DPIR PIJ JSB—KSI PZXEIL KS N DPIR SHSZJXIS
RX RSCC KS RGS RZERG SHSI NW NR AXBRB GNK GNB OXY
—BPKESC FXCLDJI

**4.4**

NSJNZX HYBYBRYH MQNM MQOX JQPSY

MQOUK JNX XMNHMYL RZ N BPGXY

—JNSM LOXUYZ

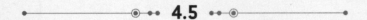

**4.5**

YJGP VJG HKTUV RWDNKEKVA ECOG QWV QP VJG VYKNKIJV

BQPG K YCU KPWPFCVGF DA UWDOKUUKQPU HTQO CIGPVU QHHGTKPI

OG UKZ HQQV PKPG CEVQTU YKVJ NQPI PGEMU VQ YJKEJ

GNGEVTQFGU EQWNF GCUKNA DG CVVCEJGF

—TQF UGTNKPI

**4.6**

YWN IQZUPE R BWU WS KWAPNX UVP

UQWOLBP ZE VPE EUOKH IZUV EW ARMX LRN RKUWQE

IVW NWMU HMWI VWI UW CBRX SOMMX

—YRQQZEWM HPZBBWQ

**4.7**

YZCF ICSK OQFY YZCGYV QMP KCSSCQM LQSSDGF BCYZ

YZDY HCML QI KQMPV C OQXSL ZDJP CMJDLPL FQKP OQXMYGV

—OSCMY PDFYBQQL

## 4.8

WL HRI RKKNHZNZ VX MFF IQN ZCLV VFRHZN GRJNP VNAMCPN
W JHRE WL HRI ZCLV MHZ W MFPR JHRE IQMI WL HRI VFRHZN
—ZRFFX TMUIRH

## 4.9

AE NADTY TVQXMQY RQM RDBRUY WMQU LDMRE A
YKJB KJB XANNALVDC AC AY REX BKRC R TMYYU
CKAES AC AY CJ PADD R TRE
—RDNQMX KACLKLJLP

## 4.10

LQEPC ESP QTWX HLD ZGPC DZXPZYP
DFRRPDEPO ESLE XLJMP XRX DSZFWO CPBFTCP
LY TB EPDE MPQZCP LWWZHTYR APZAWP TYEZ ESP
ESPLEPC T NLY FYOPCDELYO ESLE
AZTYE ZQ GTPH TQ APZAWP OZ YZE SLGP ESP
NZFCEPDJ EZ DSFE FA OFCTYR L QTWX
ESPJ DSZFWO LE WPLDE MP DPRCPRLEPO TYEZ
DAPNTLW DLEFCOLJ VTOOTP XLETYPPD YZ
XLEEPC SZH LOGLYNPO ESPTC JPLCD
—CZRPC PMPCE

# 4.11

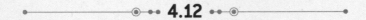

TCOATGOWC ZTC HVRITOC ENTGHSHQ GNH AOCP WK ATC
ZTC ZWCZHOSH GNOB KTZOIOGJ ATFHB OG GNH AWBG SHQBTGOIH
TCP HVRIOZOG AHTCB WK ZWAAXCOZTGOWC JHG PHSOBHP KWQ
YXOZF ATBB TRRQHZOTGOWC
—ETIG POBCHJ

# 4.12

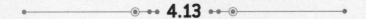

ZDYQLHYT IJYE AJYEZWR NJWYRTJCJYZWY XK QWY
FLRTJCYMT FMJYDLCYQLHYQLHYE QYT IJY YDCJWTYWR CRY
FQYELEJFRYQLHYMTLLWJYDLCYRTZWYRTZFOYKJYM XXYD
ZXHCJYZWYFLRYRTJYD XXZFOYALKFYUHRYRTJYWR QZFOYALKF
—E CQYBZMNDLCA

# 4.13

WDVDLOPOHTIOPIWBDIEOYPWIWYXVUIMD
HZYQWOZIZXVWXYDIWBDIEOYPWIZXVWXYDIQLQOVQSVDIWHIDLDYUSH
MUIQTMIDTWOYDVUICHLDYTDMISUINBQWIWBDIGDHGVDINQTWIWBDI
HPWIWDYYOEUOTCIWBOTCIOPINBQWIGDHGVDIMHINQTW
—ZVOLDISQY TDP

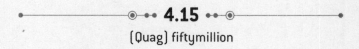

## 4.14
### (Quag) barefootonthe

```
INLXJ  AALQD  JBETJ  EGONY  EHFLO  OYEHT  JZBGR  EFUWO  YIXBI
NIBTW  PLRYM  RGNLR  XHWGS  XKOZU  SSXAR  MTBOO  JBIWH  FGXYC
UINLP  MRUQE  YKYAG  DRIOO  PDREY  OBQDX  NJBOD  TLUOK  BAHH
```

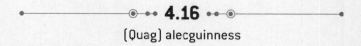

## 4.15
### (Quag) fiftymillion

```
NSVJM  OGJRP  MBNWJ  LRQRO  JLXCX  RYFCY  ASPTV  VNMLG  BZQVW
YDCGZ  STRAW  VBPTL  WYKDF  LFTAH  WRGYN  YDANH  PCCBR  OWKQN
KSVPM  IQCPC  MGWIT  OYZQV  JTABM  JKPXB  EDLQR  SIDGS  XLPPR
MFARZ  RQFLU  ZCPNX  AXLVC  LRJPR  ZNEJM  JAREJ  JKFSE  JAURS
                        GSEJA  UEUJ
```

## 4.16
### (Quag) alecguinness

```
XSZNV  THKYZ  PNEPG  KZRGV  BKDMH  BJMBE  YLIBB  KRSQY  DOKZZ
RWZUG  GTRVB  BPQDF  IMIMS  SQZDL  FLMOI  MDOWQ  TIVSM  YMGAV
BAGBM  IPTKJ  VHIUH  VMTPI  YUOIL  ULZKE  LRUHT  XHMQT  VHGBR
YLVFY  ODQRZ  VQNEE  JTTBL  SVHVF  YLATU  MDBAR  SRWVG  MSVMC
EAOYV  CNLYM  QZQYY  PPQMM  JLYFE  VTVTB  AMDPH  SIPWB  NSVSK
                 FZUAR  UOSSH  VKAXG  DF
```

## 4.17
### (Quag) nittygritty

```
TJWBA VUSTJ CTPHQ JCTPJ ENGUS RVLSE LHPWO TWHQM IAPNO
MCSUA GFKEC PVJSY ZNRBX HRCDC YLSRY MMYGE EQJYS XEYRG
TABFK WUATE CVLOW MKWHL BJRCE VTQOC CCQPY SNSYM FSVNH
CTYYK DWOWT ATUXZ ASVLR YDSEK GZWRY CKWJS QCFYA UTQSY
SFRYR VURPF SDEBF HAXHR YMWHE ONHSE RNRHP YXVOK TECMX
      CXTPV FCZYU CYWOH GCTQH HZKDP OITJR ZGG
```

## 4.18
### (Quag) betweenturning

```
NQSIG USRSX IWTSL PWDLU YTQLE ZVEOY XVZOD PUXYQ UXXUX
KDXEX ZWRQV LWAAD ASSXN ZDROO VSVRJ DVWPW DHDHO TKDDN
XQTVZ ZUALG KFROO THEEX QNXVA IAQEZ CEFNM NBFHK DXXRA
      AYXUF NWWYA ZDATV BYOAJ UNFY
```

## 4.19
### (Quag) childrenfrom

```
JXXKI MYFIP HURXK WAYIG IQPYR HZZFQ LHJKI DVTUM OIMNZ
ZEYBZ YQHKR NBZPP QZEII YNZUU SVXMB USVQY EUTYK SEXSS
PPKIT IZZYU GPSXZ RAAKJ BWUVK IEUXY MOTHX YUDXY SDLHO
ZEPYP KUXPQ CONMR SYEEF ANSTP NKREX CNCFT EWYSA NTXHA
      RKKYT PUNFO HMIMW CN
```

## 4.20

(Quag) interestingthing

```
KKMGI DGZIK OFCZR AQFKK OVWGF PTGIW FBWDN JWBIH SJTRS
VAMKT MFMBF EKNWP UFTYE XJNOD NJWBI XDPPQ TANJT NIQDC
BPOQG KMZWQ OFPEJ PMWTB IGMNF QDALJ HHCXW MFCTK VXTFD
AGKUF MSMGM PSHXG DGMAL JMZZA MTUBI QVXKK QALPP DOUIF
VETQS NFFJR VJFKZ VSNFH ORDXD ZHYVX BKCQO BVGIV AB
```

## 4.21

(Play) goldenstatuette

```
AJMESHUTVTNFRBAJDYSYDGUROYDGUWBTRCNTAVGJICNUDYUWBT
PAJGCDUTLMVTHSBRGPFGPLDVHSYMIFASVJCJUSTIBCDFDGCUYM
EKAFBFKYYGVJDGMSSAGSJIFERCNTAVRJARMDKDHPAFBFKYYGUC
SNICIFFEMSCNDZEISLZAGRPAECGTEFCDUTULBLLBDFPAUKPAJL
JCHLBCGDAI
```

## 4.22

(Play) philadelphia

```
XPMUBSMNXPEDZEPVNSNVCWACIAAGCYREOARADNAMPJMDECAVGO
IOMKMICLYCMOCUGBLCMETNMNRUUNONIRTUGBUJONLRAGUMWMSN
NUJOIPHJRVWSZKMWMUNMSBVCYCBDFDPBMAHBHPBXOW
```

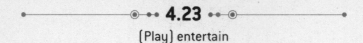

## 4.23

(Play) entertain

ZCHZCRYVZJOMPFVYCRZMJZOEJWRAENMVCKOKPVJVSEMIUMRHWU
KAVCZBZBKRYFVOUCORVBKORCST

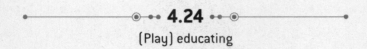

## 4.24

(Play) educating

AHMBGNFWNWBYOMDMTAWBJKEOBRTDNWTAXBOABLMATCMJXBPOBK
MCBGBLTBRHMOEBRCFBRCFBTRIMMAMEGMFEFMCIMUPTCZBJMARI
ZG

## 4.25

TE OI SR TE NY UI ES HR YU AG OT RN AD PL UY US LW
LR GR HM VE AE HO LB SN SW EE OC NO UF OT NA PA DO
RE FI LO ES

## 4.26

YU NW HT OR RB EI IS HT OH VN SE EO GM VE AL FI ER
DL SR AS EE IT EO IS TV MR IO KO WA YU PO LM ST TA
YU AE TE NN UH OI SL OL FS ID EA EN WR DN HM VE SE
EA TN

## 4.27

```
SI NI TA EO PA NN TA TE ED NS UM VE HW DN SU SI HE
US HD DT VL EO AO HR IL OY AS HY EF AD HM VE IL IE
IS MS AE IP ES OW AA OT HF CT AT EI OA RA EI GN AD
AC NJ YE OC ET SS RC ML II GH TH NW IO AR OI SO SI
OA RW TL MR WO IN EO VF RN TE ML IN ER TE RA RI TE
OI WL GV KD AI TK NM RS IN HT BU TE AT HT HD NS US
                RS NI GN DN IG AL NW
```

## 4.28

```
IORT MFSY LOHO NSNU DROR ALTL KSME FEAN HAPO ESIA
LAIR MEAH SETI LITH FIRE BRNW OHNK YHTU ANHU FAOM
DTOE HINX EFMI TNFA IRWE DIYO THSF EAHE TGYN TWAR
     GALH AEDF OICO CIFE DDIT SELT SLGE ILBA
```

## 4.29

```
Z OWQA LA BWRC PAC CW COA QWZRC LOAKA LA OJDA CW
OJDA COA VJC MCWQ VOJMZRP COA UWIMA CW CAJVO OZU
       PYJMMEYWLZRP JRB EJMXAC LAJDZRP
              —TWMAQO EJKEAKJ
```

## 4.30

### (Quag) sammydavis

SYZKG ZAZVZ KYFJR YANGA EZZEO AOEGQ GXGCJ DWQKM CIORE
EFANO GDYFH TUFZT FUJXY ZCFFK WZZPA ZZNCS CLQZE ZQUMG
AECTO AZSPR OFFHF OMKIG GFOOS TDLIT HCKYL HUJEJ VVJXC
FNMGI ZRKJU JWRRE OMCYB

## 4.31

### (Quag) facelift

AFMEO PEKAJ MOLRN WFITO VCKFQ NRECY EKVFP FZSHO KOQAF
EUHRV BJVIW OAEJY KGRFH HEITZ FPFKV OLHQH WGKWC XHIMU
TDMEX MPEYX EH

## 4.32

ZNF XSKVXZFU PXQZEES KL ICLZ XMECZ ZNF GCQFLZ TFXLZ
XQDCXMTF VELZ KSWKDEQXZKSD XQZ HEQV KSWFSZFU LKSPF
VXSOKSU UKU LNXUEJ LNEJL JKZN JQKDDTKSD HKSDFQL
—QXA MQXUMCQA

## 4.33

ON IMKC ORC TNENOC X BNND NH XYOMTMAXONQE ZCBMIRO M
ZQXP CKCQEORMYI SA ORC CECJ XQC SA ORC CXQJ XQC SA XYZ
CKCY ORC YNJC MJ SA PRCY RC MJ ZCHCXOCZ NY ORC NORCQ
RXYZ CKCQEORMYI OSQYJ ZNPY

—TRSTD FNYCJ

## 4.34

R PFGI ID YFQL IYL NWG DN TDRGU FGREL FGT R BDQL FGREL
AWI R VFGI TD HIDKSADFKTH ALVFWHL R VFGI KLFBBS TKFP
FGT IYFIH PYFI IYLS BRQL FGT TRL DG

—XWLGIRG IFKFGIRGD

## 4.35

DMPUA UE M YQPUGY AR QZFQDFMUZYQZF ITUOT BQDYUFE
YUXXUAZE AR BQABXQ FA XUEFQZ FA FTQ EMYQ VAWQ NF FTQ
EMYQ FUYQ MZP KQF DQYMUZ XAZQEAYQ

—FE QXUAF

## 4.36

E IUXR AN FRQEPR BN SPNXR UAVBIEAJ DV FUAHEAJ E IUXR
ARXRP TQRF EB UQ UA NTBWRB NP U LRUAQ NM RZSPRQQEAJ
LVQRWM E YTQB FUAHR E YTQB STB LV MRRB EA BIR UEP
UAF LNXR BIRL UPNTAF

—MPRF UQBUEPR

# • • GIRL CRAZY • •

Here's a cryptogram that, although definitely not in Russian, uses the Russian alphabet. Solve it symbolically. We'll give you a hint. The very first letter represents the letter H.

# ЗДММ ЗАФЗ ОП ЕХТЩ

# МИЛД ФЗД МАЧЩДТ ПЕ

# А ЧПНАО УВПТОДГ

38

# FOOD & DRINK

"AS A CHILD MY FAMILY'S MENU CONSISTED
OF TWO CHOICES: TAKE IT OR LEAVE IT."
—*Buddy Hackett*

## 5.1

T GR MRV ITLW JXRBBRIT UMG T SUNWMV ITLWG TV

OTMBW T QUO U ITVVIW LTG UMG KD KRVSWX KUGW KW WUV TV

UMG TK ZXWOTGWMV RP VSW CMTVWG OVUVWO UMG TK MRV YRTMY

VR WUV UMD KRXW JXRBBRIT

—YWRXYW JCOS

## 5.2

LGPMC QPSU XMEUY PY BFVN LGUPYFSU PY P VIYWGH RMUW

ONMGU DSUPR PCR OPWUS VICQUS WNU NMXNUYW LIYYMDGU

LGUPYFSU ONUC WNUH PSU DSIFXNW WI NFCXSH GMLY

—ULMVFSFY

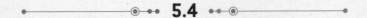

## 5.3

Y OFXX UYCT OEFD TEPMXC OEVPH WHWD OEF BFVFWX
WRC FWO OEF KPZ WO XFWTO OEFDC IFO TPLF SYKFV

—VYBEWVC EPXTOFYR

## 5.4

LWJZ YWKN TY V UDMC EMTLSC EITFR VFZ TE TY
EID MVMD IWYEDYY OIW LVF LVMMC TE WQQ AWMD WQEDF
EIVF FWE EID ZTFFDM RKDYE TY JDQE OTEI EID
TANMDYYTWF EIVE IVZ ID WFJC LWAD V JTEEJD DVMJTDM
ID LWKJZ IVUD RWEEDF TE OITJD TE OVY YETJJ IWE

—QMVF JDPWOTEX

## 5.5

PAO UOBP ZKC PS RSBO ZOVJAP VB PS ERSBO CSMQ
GSMPA BSGOPAVFJ NOQC TVYYVEMRP YSQ K WSRVPVEVKF
SQ ZKPEA CSMQ YSST LMBP ZKPEA VP TSFP OKP VP

—OTZKQT XSEA

## 5.6

LW RBVUBP UBFR LC UB KUBT AGOXMS XMUXLGUC RXMMCPK
DBP DBQP QMFCKK UACPC GPC UAPCC BUACP TCBTFC

—BPKBM ICFFCK

## 5.7

KFT AIPM VZM KA JTTY MARO FTZPKF LE
KA TZK VFZK MAR BAIK VZIK BOLIJ VFZK MAR
BAIK PLJT ZIB BA VFZK MARB OZKFTO IAK
—NZOJ KVZLI

## 5.8

GPUE CGY DRRZXRRZB CYUU TRQ GRH CR DRRZ CGY ERRF
CGY RCGYS GPUE CYUU TRQ GRH CR PJRVF YPCVKL VC
—PKFT SRRKYT

## 5.9

RKQOYAULMLOU SLOOIXA RQYI ILUKRIIO KJHXA RJ FXIFQXI
RKIZ QXI GJOAHPIS LO RNICMI PLOHRIA KQCE-RLPIA RQYI
RNICMI PLOHRIA RKLA LA OJR GJLOGLSIOGI
—IXPQ DJPDIGY

## 5.10

(Play) differentkinds

DHXEPTQPXGEXSHEVXVJQGJQPXYXJILYHXFQDHUXDRXZEIHUXEPXEKT
XEAAQPXDGXAEETXEAXTDAAQPQHGXSDHTRXYGXRJEPGXDHGQPBYKRXD
AXZEIHUXDGXVDKKXQYGXYHZGJDHUXYGXYHZXJEIPXEAXGJQXTYZXEP
XHDUJGXDAXEKTXDGXEFRQPBQRXRGYGQTXMQPDETRX
—EKDBQPXVQHTQ KKXJEKLQR

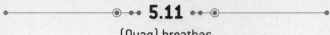

## 5.11

### (Quag) breathes

```
ASQHM XPOTR FTHNU EKSQB DEFRA NMNYT CIPFI
HWBQZ FTIXA PSXLN ANQRC Y3TMF CQQEM
```

## 5.12

### (Play) tokeepacow

```
PJDUSERKECTZXSUTPSGBGSBORPJSESXTJSTRDLUPMSLHBUGBJS
TRKRGUCOKDSAGBBJUACUPDSJSJTBKDDWBLUPNPPJSXPJFDUPUK
DUMDPVTPJSSXESSYPJCLKRGJTRSFKEJGKEMYSNDZMPBLNBPRLT
KEESUMBL
```

## 5.13

```
DN TK AU CE SD IE NO TC OM AI HK EH DE CE AD RO EO
TA EB TH RA VC OH WO OK ET FE NW EB AH FN YO NY
```

## 5.14

```
EI EFRLSU HNM N JFFG USVUSNRPFTNY VFFB AOR HLNR MLS
ANMPVNYYI ASYPSZSG NAFOR VFFBPTJ HNM RLNR PC IFO HFUBSG
LNUG NTG QUFMQSUSG MFESFTS SYMS HFOYG GF PR CFU IFO
—TFUN SQLUFT
```

## 5.15

NBY BCABQUS CM LYJFYNY QCNB WOFCHULS FUHX GCFYM
XCMAOCMYX UM KOUCHN FIWUF LYMNUOLUHNM NBUN WULLS MOWB
LYUMMOLCHA HUGYM UM GCFFCYM JIJM UHX WUJNH XCWEM

—VLSUH GCFFYL

## 5.16

RB LPF AWIIMF OMFBWB SRFJRFNCM
N IFWBI XPHB SPFM IGRC XGMSNBIB

—EPRC JWBBPH

## 5.17

(Quag) livingliquid

FVLOE SPYTB ECLYT YTKNR YJNFU NTJVC ZBJOM HKFOA EURDT
AMNUT QNYGX SPWIQ KVBOM EZKCQ IFDKJ RNEZY NMVHP NMKBF
DUEQB CMACA UHPEQ KPKDU JOZSZ NOFHH KSBXB GDVCC ENXDT
NGHMQ LKXKR WIUEF QUTUX

## 5.18

(Quag) penicillin

HOHGN WEHTD INSDQ IKHCT MRZUF IRFCL UILDV SHFIR AVLKV
HWSDQ GVINZ FLKXG ZXCCI CFODI JKJID RPFDR RFUHJ TUQEF
L

```
G ACFFXF LGB UDXGNNMDJZ DZ LGB YF UPRR DZ LGB YF
JGDHF DZ LGB YF MHFQXMNCDXZDAGZFU BFZ DZ QFLGDJX
      ACFFXF LDROX RFGN ZMSGQU DLLMQZGRDZB
                —ARDVZMJ VGUDLGJ
```

## • • *BOUNCEBACK CIPHER* • •

This is a simple code. The letters of each word are fractionated into multiple groupings, going alternately from left to right. The word CHRISTMAS would look like this

```
CRSMS ATIH
```

*then split into 3 groups:*

```
CRS    MSA    TIH
```

You can "bunch" letters together in groups of 3, 4, 5, and so on. Here's a quotation for you to decode.

```
AYN    WOA    SHH    EON
NVR    AEM    IAD    MEE
SAE    ANV    EES    HKT
RRE    AYH    ITN    DIT
NNW                  EG

—ABR   ENT    IN  ESI  TEL
```

# GREAT MINDS

"GENIUS IS MORE OFTEN FOUND IN A CRACKED POT THAN IN A WHOLE ONE." —*E.B. White*

## 6.1

KUFLCFLV FX KUA UQZJAXK GHZC KUAZA FX GUFEU

FX KUA DZHRQRMA ZAQXHL GUN XH OAG ALVQVA FL FK

—UALZN OHZJ

## 6.2

SLCG DPQTLCP CMBPGEKZF YMPCZG YM UETG IML

OWTZZPY KG GM YM YMPCZG BPTZ KGC LCPWPCC

—GEMBTC TWRT PYKCMZ

## 6.3

BORFGYK WRFO FSY VIGPSJO R KOYJZOWRY

AOZGOLGYK DCRJ CO BORF WRFO CGW WRF

—KOSBKO AOBYRBF NCRD

## 6.4

EAK EKSX AJUN XEL HUK HUWWX ARNJ XEL

OKEA SUKBLUBD OKEA HELKNWRDI OKEA VDEVSD

SDN XELW FDFEWX MD XELW NWUTDS MUB

—USDPUKQDW IESGJDKRNIXK

## 6.5

L CN CW CZWADHLM L XA WAH IYJHJWX HA

GWAB BPCH NCWE LZWAYCWH NJW CYJ DFYJ AS

—MTCYJWMJ XCYYAB

## 6.6

UBUGZHWNZ OUVK KW QMXC ETSWGQFVEWT FJJ

NFZ JWTO VCFV VCUZ JWKU VCUEG XWQQWT KUTKU

—OUGVGMNU KVUET

## 6.7

IS SIF TKI DF K UJFKH HOLIRFJ EOS XSFG ISH JFTSUILCF

HOKH KG K HOLIRFJ LH LG OLG VLJGH XBHQ HS VSYYSE OLG

LIHFYYFTH HS EOKHFPFJ TSITYBGLSIG LH WKQ YFKX

—ZSOI GHBKJH WLYY

## 6.8

MO XCQ JTDV VC MDBNMPW ZCDOMHWDZW IMYW
NKWDVX CO BVTVMBVMZB MV HCWB DCV FTVVWP VETV
VEWX BECQKH AW TZZQPTVW CP WYWD MDVWKKMIMAFW
TB KCDI TB VEWPW MB WDCQIE CO VEWF

—KWJMB ZTPPCKK

## 6.9

YA YP IQERUZ IGRAYRTYRU IQERUZ YRZOYAELSZ IQERLZ AQEA
YP AQZ HGBYRERA CEIAGD YR PGIYZAN AGHEN AQYP YR ATDR
BZERP AQEA GTD PAEAZPBZR GTD LTPYRZPPBZR GTD ZOZDNBER
BTPA AEFZ GR E PIYZRIZ
CYIAYGRES MEN GC AQYRFYRU

—YPEEI EPYBGO

## 6.10

YIMO OTZZ XTIXZT FIP OI YI OFUMDC OTZZ OFTK PFBO
OI YI BMY ZTO OFTK CLVXVUCT GIL PUOF OFTUV VICLZOC

—DTIVDT C XBOOIM

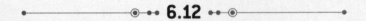
ZFW ZFKOSI ZFLZ TKBB NWIZCRE YI LCW ARBKZKGI

TKZFRYZ ACKOGKABW ABWLIYCW TKZFRYZ GROIGKWOGW

TWLBZF TKZFRYZ TRCV VORTBWNSW TKZFRYZ GFLCLGZWC

XYIKOWII TKZFRYZ PRCLBKZE IGKWOGW TKZFRYZ

FYPLOKZE LON TRCIFKA TKZFRYZ ILGCKHKGW

—PLFLZPL SLONFK

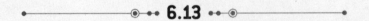
HWGPKORM TGN HKW KGDUWNH TZDE O KGU WAWD UZRW

GRU OH DWCGORN HKW KGDUWNH TZDE O KGAW UZRW HZ UGHW

—GRR DOPKGDUN

VKRZ YT CR F AIHHU ZK GKRVTJR YTGFIMT AT VKTMRZ VK

OAFZ UKI VK KH ZACRP FM UKI ZACRP KH FM NFMZ ZATHT OFM

F ZCJT OATR UKI VCVRZ PRKO OAFZ UKI PRKO ZKVFU

—JFXGKXJ B

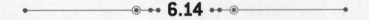
C ZIVD XVFMG LGTSO CR T RLVFJTIO RCYGJ PGWVSG

PFR CRJ RSFG LTSO DVSZ KTXJ VWW CW XVF DTIR RV PG

QVVO XVF LTMG RV KSTURCUG KSTURCUG KSTURCUG CW

XVF OVIR AVMG JVYGRLCIQ RLGI OVIR OV CR

—STX PSTOPFSX

## 6.15

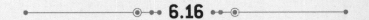

IBJX JZQSI IXXJ KFJBIR RB AWXKRX RYXJIXFLXI IEWZQHZQH
TE TQSXW XLXWN SZIKSLKQRKHX KQS UBWOZQH RYXZW IBFZRKWN
GTR ZWWXIZIRZGFX UKN RYWBTHY K RYBTIKQS BGIRKAFXI
—UKIYZQHRBQ ZWLZQH

## 6.16

HBUBX CKAFN NGEN E LIEPP JXKAY KS NGKAJGNSAP
MKIIQNNBC MQNQOBHL MEH MGEHJB NGB VKXPC QHCBBC
QNL NGB KHPT NGQHJ NGEN BUBX GEL
—IEXJEXBN IBEC

## 6.17

NMMY RLRH CXSG YMSYOM LVS AXH AS KMOFAAOM HSWX
RGKFAFSTE EGROO YMSYOM ROLRHE IS AVRA KWA AVM XMROOH
ZXMRA GRNM HSW CMMO AVRA HSW ASS URT KMUSGM ZXMRA
—GRXN ALRFT

## 6.18

PYBH X PSR S RISKK ZVW LUVPXHL EG XH CSHRSR S JUXBHT
VJ IXHB SHT X PBHD JXRYXHL SHT SR PB RSD DYBUB XH DYB
PSUIDY VJ S REIIBU SJDBUHVVH VH S UXABUZSHC PB DSKCBT
SZVED PYSD PB PSHDBT DV TV PYBH PB LUBP EG X DVKT YXI
DYSD X PSHDBT DV ZB S UBSK ISOVU KBSLEB ZSRBZSKK
GKSWBU S LBHEXHB GUVJBRRXVHSK KXCB YVHER PSLHBU IW
JUXBHT RSXT DYSD YBT KXCB DV ZB GUBRXTBHD VJ DYB
EHXDBT RDSDBR HBXDYBU VJ ER LVD VEU PXRY
—TPXLYD TSAXT BXREHYVPBU

## 6.19

SEVSG ZX OZIN LOO ANLVSZYVO SGZMPX ZM SGN UJEOT
ZS TJNX MJS TZXROJXN ZSX TNXZELAZOZSW NFRNQS
SJ SGJXN UGJ YZEXS YNNO SGN
ZMYOVNMRN JY YLOXNGJJT
—ILGOZO PZAELM

## 6.20

WVQAHJQ PWV AMPHRM WVBTQ YEWY UO MWOQ ALY
YH AM WVBTQ DUYE YEM TUBEY CMTOHV WVJ YH YEM TUBEY
JMBTMM WVJ WY YEM TUBEY YURM WVJ SHT YEM TUBEY
CLTCHOM WVJ UV YEM TUBEY DWQ YEWY UO VHY DUYEUV
MNMTQAHJQO CHDMT WVJ UO VHY MWOQ
—WTUOYHYFM

WIVV JGVVTY ZJ KF R XIVRK GVFGCV NYRK

NZEUJ RIV KF FTVREJ REU DRCRIZRC IVXZFEJ NYZTY

NRWK RNRP KYV VCVDVEKJ FW UZJVRJV REU SIZEX

EVN VCVDVEKJ FW YVRCKY REU NYVIV WIVV JGVVTY ZJ

JKFGGVU DZRJDR ZJ SIVU REU UVRKY TFDVJ WRJK

—YVEIP NRIU SVVTYVI

6.22

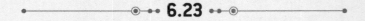

Y TE DEJ VUUB ERBYWUT JE RUBYULU JXQJ JXU ICCU

WET MXE UDTEMUT KI MYJX IUDIU HUQIED QDT YDJUEBUSJ

XQI YDJUDTUT KI JE VEHWE JXUYH KIU

—WQBYBUE WQBYBUY

6.23

KV KU VJG JGKIJV QH CDUWTFKVA VQ UQY NKVVNG DWV

YGGFU KP VJG HKTUV JCNH QH QPGU NKHGVKOG CPF GZRGEV

VQ JCTXGUV C XCNWCDNG ETQR KP VJG UGEQPF JCNH

—RGTEA LQJPUVQP

## 6.24

ZKDVSD FRA YQDVC AV J
WZFVKOCFDQLVZRVZKDVIRSQJVZKDVMASD FRA
YQDVRADVWDSFOFZFVOAVZSXOAPVZRV J
WZVZKDVIRSQJVZRVKOCFDQLVZKDSDLRSDV
QQVWSRPSDFFVJDWDAJFVRAVZKDVMASD FRA YQDVC
AVPDRSPDVYDSA SJVFK I

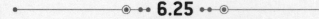

## 6.25

QZKWDSZKJZZTKPRECYHZKY
TKRIAKOCDTTZEKJAZZEYTPKRVKRIAKER
LZXGY
DGZEKOCDTGXKDTEKDTYLDCXKJ
IGKQZKWDSZKJZZTKADJJYGCYHZKYT
KRIAKITOCDTTZEKJAZZEYTPKRV
KRIAXZCSZXKDATRCEKMRXZOWKGR
UTJZZ

## 6.26

YQW WA IWYNWH GGBKW
WNJLBBJNRBBMBLWVBWNVZDGKWNRBBMWNJLBBJNWBEBIW NWAYHVBG
IPBGZWM YIJBKWZLWFBBJVZEBIWMG XEKWADNYHWZLWNV OBNMB
LBWRLZJBWMZBJLXWVBWNVZDGKWNRBBMWNJLBBJNWNZWRBGGWJV JW
GGWJVBWVZNJNWZQWVB EBIW IKWB LJVWRYGGWM DNBWJZWN
XWVBLBWGYEBKW WPLB
JWNJLBBJNRBBMBLWRVZWKYKWVYNWSZFWRBGGWA
LJYIWGDJVBLWOYIP

## 6.27

TRSGNKETMCJRSCARMSVJDSLKEVS

JKSVTBGSEJLLCMMGNSMJSLGLJO

SJOSGBGRSVJDSLKEVS

JKSYRJDSCMASZGCRFSTZQGSMJSNCUUGOGRMCTMGSZGMDGGRSDVTMS

JKSNJSYRJDSTRNSDVTMS JKSNJRMS

—TRTMJQGSUOTREG

## 6.28

(Quag) conventional

MUPAP LLAPY MAEZO MCMVC YORZQ VOLND YJPCC YHSOM FMDYQ

MODFZ JZKUO MXWYR DOPMJ NGPIC JDRWV CALNM KKYCO TZVAH

LOWZV MMYSD POIBW AJSJK VRMIX JKEXT UZVPB AHKCK WIVAN

YKPNC ZTSMV VEQRZ QKYFF DSTII AKDKP IBCZR NGINH OKQPR

OARRL KFYCL ISJOA VXDYJ

## 6.29

(Quag) moredangerous

ZCKDV GYTYE OCQQH JBENX IVCZK TKLZG ACJWE EQVPG ZEZGN

WKOWE JLVLK KKIRR DUYRV QSXIW BFTDF CVUTT JRTUD VDTYA

WXEFC BKGGX RWKTE WDWSS KUTMD GNQFC TNOGC VSTUN QAAQE

FVCDV YIFWS XEDDA NKKFC VTQGQ DGOXR

## 6.30

### (Play) conveniences

JDTVOLUORYUAIWNARBUNTNOCRUSLDVILIWZPWGOUKCNBMLCPJY
MSBUDRDBEIKZUTZPSXACXBJDWGWNUTDBOLCKBUPGNITIGPXDMR
PBJDDRLBOPSOREUBIAPNBTLSISGWDRCKEWSUPTGJANIDKPEPMG
SDUGIDRW

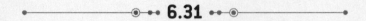

## 6.31

EPQ CQJUQQ ZB ZGQV QRZEMZG IOUMQV

MGIQUVQXF TMEP ZGQV AGZTXQCJQ ZB EPQ BOSEV

EPQ XQVV FZH AGZT EPQ PZEEQU FZH JQE

—DQUEUOGC UHVVQXX

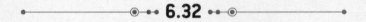

## 6.32

OFPQH RFP BCSSPO KHIHIDHK OFH

GCQO CKH BPSEHISHE OP KHGHCO ZO

—LHPKLH QCSOCXCSC

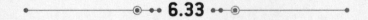

## 6.33

ORSIZAHURSYRF NUR MJIZNMXI URW

AYHOUHYMR CMGIJIZ XWAHIZYMOA

MZ YRAOZXMORHUQBI YH XUW UVVIUZ HM QI

—RMZXUR JYRNIRH VIUBI

## 6.34

```
IO ES AL LA SO SS FR NS AD IT EN UH OA NA NH TC NI
ET EO TN IB EF LT TE TE HR CE OA HN SM NE RE AH NT
NH PI HL AW YP SE SI ME SN VR UE OG TM IT IW AI OS
DR HM SE VA LO AL IL SH CA AT RF NO ET AG OG WS IG
                         OJ
```

## 6.35

```
HS OY SH VR IN FA TV NS HT EP EA EE IE TA RE PN AO
EN OA AT IT RI TE ES OO PS EE TT AP OL HV DC DD OG
              EU ON PL OB NP RE
```

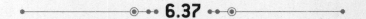

## 6.36

```
GD LN KO SH FT RB TN YN IT RA CN LE TE AT MR SB EC
OA OE NW TE UU EU OL AH SO IN AA TR HP SA BO EI RE
```

## 6.37

```
         SLR VZ YOT BRCA JDTLYFDT YOLY JBRZFSTZ
        PVYOBFY KDBQFJVRX OT QBTZ RBY XVUT SVCH OT
          QBTZ RBY CLA TXXZ OT VZ YBB PTLH YB KFCC
       YOT KCBFXO OT JLRRBY DFR WLZY TRBFXO YB JLYJO
        DLMMVYZ ATY OT VZ CBDQ BW LCC YOT LRVSLCZ
              —XTBDXT BDPTCC
```

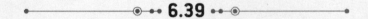

IKHDPMOHIKHUFNHZPCDGHKFIDDHDIKUHUFNCNHZSDDHJNHZCPMOKHI

MGHS

HMPHLIMHPJVNEUNGHIMGHMPHLIMHCNJNDDNGHUFPKNHZCPMOKHZPWD

GHDIKUH PCNYNCH

—EDICNMENHGICCPZ

GEMWHYKDNKTMGMYKGZKOEHPLFDSHKJDUZGEXKMRFKRMEEZVK

DRFHFRHNNKMRFK

MRXKZTKZLEKOHZOYHKRHHFKDGKNZEHYXKZRKGIHNHKMSSZLRGNKJEZ

MFKVIZYHNZ HKSIMEDGMJYHKWDHVNKZTK

HRKMRFKGIDRUNKSMRRZGKJHKMSBLDEHFKJXKWHUHGMGDRUKDRKZRHK

YDGGYHKSZERHEKZTKGIHKHMEGIKMYYKZRHNKYDTHGD H

—MEAKGVMDR

(Quag) ofamerica

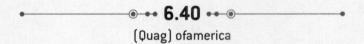

ERPIZ RPEUT OICNJ PSJFJ PNRSM ACZGD RMBFW TMXLE SNLRP

OQDRI MCORH TGKAQ HANPO XKHFR BJVQR TVOPU LZKQC AJMQX

UCTQT DRQAN RQFDO RDTAW CNBMC JYHFO PATER FBL

W OA GCASVCK ZSGG WBHSFSGHSR WB HVS KSWUVH OBR

QCBJCZIHWCBG CT SWBGHSWBG PFOWB HVOB WB HVS BSOF

QSFHOWBHM HVOH DSCDZS CT SEIOZ HOZSBH VOJS ZWJSR

OBR RWSR WB QCHHCB TWSZRG OBR GKSOHGVCDG

—GHSDVSB XOM UCIZR

## • • *POLYBIUS CHECKERBOARD* • •

This is another code first proposed by Polybius around 150 B.C.E. It's contained in a 5x5 grid where the letters Y and Z share the same grid. Replace each letter with the row and column number in which it appears (row first, then column).

|   | 1 | 2 | 3 | 4 | 5 |
|---|---|---|---|---|---|
| 1 | A | B | C | D | E |
| 2 | F | G | H | I | J |
| 3 | K | L | M | N | O |
| 4 | P | Q | R | S | T |
| 5 | U | V | W | X | Y/Z |

Using this grid, the name POLYBIUS becomes

```
41 – 35 – 32 – 55 – 12 – 24 – 51 – 44
 P    O    L    Y    B    I    U    S
```

Try this one:

45-23-15-43-15-44　34-35　44-51-13-23
45-23-24-34-22　11-44　21-51-34
21-35-43 45-23-15　53-23-35-32-15
21-11-33-24-32-55

—25-15-43-43-55　44-15-24-34-21-15-32-14

# HUMOR

"NOTHING SHOWS A MAN'S CHARACTER MORE THAN WHAT HE LAUGHS AT." *—Johann Wolfgang Von Goethe*

## 7.1

UXS TFEB OVESA QTDSWB QLF UTESOLJS LOS UXTAS TH
ULAUS LFW UXS TFEB EKDKULUKTFA UXTAS TH EKPSE

—YLDSA UXVOPSO

## 7.2

IFP RAYI XPRVXZVGDP IFHWS VGAQI RN RAIFPX HY IFVI
CAX IFHXIN NPVXY YFP YPXUPM IFP CVRHDN WAIFHWS GQI
DPCIAUPXY IFP AXHSHWVD RPVD FVY WPUPX GPPW CAQWM

—KVDUHW IXHDDHW

## 7.3

ERW NEMEGNEGTN DB NMBGES MCW ERME DBW
DAE DY WQWCS YDAC MPWCGTMBN GN NAYYWCGBL YCDP
NDPW YDCP DY PWBEMI GIIBWNN ERGBU DY SDAC ERCWW
FWNE YCGWBVN GY ERWS MCW DUMS ERWB GEN SDA

—CGEM PMW FCDXB

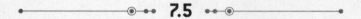

## 7.4

EXF VLHFN TFX RLAG LEV KPVT F MGK XESCGN
FWWFSGMVON VTSGG LEV LJ JLES WGLWOG AFYG EW
XGCGMVN JPCG WGSRGMV LJ VTG WLWEOFVPLM
—HFCPH OGVVGSAFM

## 7.5

BSCQHXDRN WSXOR XH QORSXWQ PQIRZ XH
BTRS KBSPL VXGGXBH NBGGQSZ Q LRQS QHN
ZURHNZ TRSL GXPPGR BH BKKXWR ZJUUGXRZ
—ABBNL QGGRH

## 7.6

SRDMD VHC H SOYD VRDA H EZZP HAB ROC YZADF VDMD
CZZA GHMSDB WNS AZV OS RHGGDAC SZ DQDMFWZBF
—HBPHO CSDQDACZA

## 7.7

SBJ JKHRZZRAATVU SBTVU TA SBRS SBJ
ARPRI IZJAATVU TA LCSUZLAATVU KE MTPKA
—NRCP VJQKRV

WS AZD ZHKZVD DFMTMWDCQ NC APK HWSSHC ZSSCYSWPY

TAWHPDPTACMD AZUC TZWQ SP AFNPM DWYOC WS WD Z NPMC

DWRYWXWOZYS TMPOCDD PX NWYQ SAZY NCZDPY NCZDPY OZY

PYHV DPMS PFS TCMOCTSWPYD IFS SAC AFNPM TMPOCDD

WD WYUPHUCQ WY OAZYRWYR SACN

—CQKZMQ QC IPYP

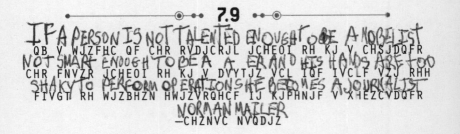

QB V WJZFHC QF CHR RVDJCRJL JCHEOI RH KJ V CHSJDQFR

CHR FNVZR JCHEOI RH KJ V DVYTJZ VCL IQF IVCLF VZJ RHH

FIVGT RH WJZBHZN HWJZVRQHCF IJ KJPHNJF V XHEZCVDQFR

—CHZNVC NVQDJZ

MSC AVFNMC MSYM ETN UCYK HTACMSVFI MSYM

ETN RYFM NFKCUHMYFK ETN RYF YBATHM JC HNUC

VM DYH KUYDF NZ JE Y BYDECU

—DVBB UTICUH

LD TKBKESWFCB PSXKU SJ FW TEKV VFWO S XOCFKK

AKWVKKB EKZFTFCMJ AKZFKP SBU KNFJWKBWFSZ UKJRSFE

XOCJK LSEFQMSBS BCV VK SEK FB CME XSAKEBKW JWSTK

—RKTTD BCCBSB

SLA TL ALSS FVB ZVTLAOPUN AOHA DL PZYHLSPZ OHCL

HNHPUZA TVZLZ OL AVVR BZ MVYAF FLHYZ AOYVBNO AOL

KLZLYA PU VYKLY AV IYPUN BZ AV AOL VUL ZWVA PU

AOL TPKKSL LHZA AOHA OHZ UV VPS

—NVSKH TLPY

OG W VOJS RWGQCJSFSR PM SLOAWBWBU AM DOGH W GHOFHSR

CIH OG O QVWZR QCWBQWRSBHOZZM GC RWR AM PFCHVSF AM

ACHVSF RWR BCH DIH OZZ VSF SUUG WB CBS POGYSH GC HC

GDSOY GVS UOJS AS O MCIBUSF PFCHVSF BOASR FIGGSZZ KVC

HOIUVH AS KVOH KOG ASOBH PM GIFJWJOZ CT HVS TWHHSGH

—PWZZ QCGPM

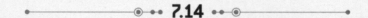

YPCQNRBRNSYEQZKQPAURXQOCSXF QYZQOZJCQZXCQRXZYPCJQ CCU

QYZQOCQWR

YDEQFJCRYCJQYPRXQYPRYQZKQRXEQZYPCJQRXSURDQ

—PQDQUCXNHCX

## 7.15

HJWOHSWGHZSXHTXWX

PWUHGMXOHLASXWXJWSXGZXVZJ

FASTWGAXKHJXBZEXYKWGXKAXHTXSZ

GXWSIXWXTASTAXZBXKPJZEXYWTXFEZLHIAIXGZXVZSTZUAXK-IJXBZE

XYKWGXKAXHTXZTVWEXYHUIA

## 7.16

OPIUXFOYXJYQVIYFLHRQUSY

VIUIYSLHYEHSYOYAXKIQXPIYJHBBASYLKYOJBXUXRYKLUYLRIYCLAA

OUYORCYHJIYXQYHBYXRYQ LY IIZJ

—TLVRYEOUUSPLUI

## 7.17

ZUDUXJCHDWZUUWCDUX WCRUDUFDHCCDGNXUDZHD

RICQDFRCHDRFHCDXDPFFIDICXWDFLDZUDUFDJRFGDZRDGNXUDIZQCA

UZFRDUFDVFZRUDUNXUDFQPXRDGDNDX ICR

## 7.18

GBETLQEUPMJEGAMLZCEPMEGMHQVJEJL EGJEGBETLQEUPMJEJL

EGJEVPQASEGJELBBEPMIEGBETLQEUPMJEVPQASEGJELBBEGJHE

ZLXPXVTEICHCZOCIE

—ZQHHCVVEVTMCH

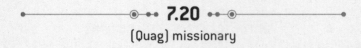

(Quag) typicaltriumph

```
MEOGU  GXLBV  NXBRB  GREIL  ABLLW  PRDJM  LHJWW  LEFKF  GNYJC
KTRCD  CWANE  DXLOW  DLJDC  LRFWA  LFLZU  XOAFG  HYLWP  QMMQJ
IXLLS  ZZHOE  LBVMJ  XGLZQ  XVJKD  PTRGD  UODHM  KYBQA  UISYC
LRIRI  AAAHX  WWCUM  IBRMJ  KLRFW  EXVOW  ZQHAM  UIFLA  XLKZI
       QWRFW  AIYKA  AOEFX  QL
```

**7.20**

(Quag) missionary

```
CCNZP  PBQSJ  VPXOT  TXDPT  SFYFU  FHYAI  AROXN  WOOXX  AFDBJ
VEPTG  BBIRE  XATUX  UFSVF  NWFHO  QQKSY  UOYNA  HBABQ  XUTPU
STNAW  GESQZ  UCYUM  AZNHJ  JXKOE  DXZTW  HKCGH  RKOJJ  BFIDE
KWBOX  GSFZO  XHCFX  FDXTC  HMKYI  YTIRZ  KQXKO  CDWXC  CTUXX
EZAFH  DGWWC  CKFXI  UIOQX  YHOKO  CUGFO  GWJZE  PTGBR
```

**7.21**

(Play) firmlypacked

```
JRRCLGBDIRMJRKNJDLFWAPURYFNJGPKJY3KMRJGLNJIPIMRJGL
ALGPLCLBLUCVAPURHJKCRWOMMRJMRCKHJRIFLSSTIFBMXFRIFG
JLHKASRKCFRGNJHMLCHRLGLSSTAGUGAVIFKIWFXBSJGIIPGPNI
FMTKOFNKVKNWRW
```

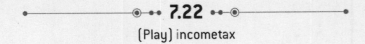

## 7.22

(Play) incometax

CWGYWUDSIYUVNHNJTOYOZWPOWUYAWVMYWGVWRYPNWYBVNHYSMO
WAWDWIUHMPTJFVWDPOWGXTBYCZPVPNZTCJIYMCEZZLLRCOFG

## 7.23

(Play) wetsidewalk

ZEHIDIHKVTFWFTVLVGOBGUBVLKCOEGBONLOCIKATVEKIBOMPXG
NKTAOVTAOVSAVTAIOBYDGCWSCEHITEENIRZEBAOETIBTCOCOAB
VHCDFGGINLORKEDFVOEIVXVGICTDFKJWTEDTAMZVLZMSTRFCVH
GW

## 7.24

IN WH AS ET EN WR IS IH NH HA TF LM NI DH AS EI TE
VI HN II TE RN BI DN CA LS CU ZK OT EN WR HA SE LE
WT IT EE RO AL AK NT EN WR SW LE TI KM NH WO GU LI
GH RE SH LO

## 7.25

GROBJQI FLD FRYB TJHM ILDAHW YDB IQRB
BLQTIQHUQI DY R IBDDH JY BLQ TJWWHQ DV BLQ VJQHW
JY LDGQI BLRB BLQ SDF FJHH NRSM AG BD BLQT
—QHNQOB LANNROW

## 7.26

KPH NAAL NO SNRWS KN KPH LKNCH ONC F

VNFO NO ICHFA FWA GNZRWS NTK YRKP NWVB F

VNFO NO ICHFA FCH KPCHH IRVVRNW KN NWH

—HCZF INZIHGJ

## 7.27

ZW FLATB TKOB KG FVKYKRE OAU YLB

MDBGYKARG YA FLKSL K LVCB IUBIVUBN VRGFBUG

—YAZ GYAIIVUN

## 7.28

U EUGH OEZWUBN HFHWVMJUIT UP UI MJH HUTJMUHP

MJH MHLCHWNMRWHP MJH NTHP NIB MJH USP

—THZWTH YNWEUI

## 7.29

BCH PSWBU OPZS HC GZSSD WG HSFFWPZS

MCI VOJS HVS AWGSFM CT VOJWBU DOFHWSR OZZ

BWUVH KWHVCIH HVS GOHWGTOQHWCB

—ZMBB XCVBGHCB

# ••COLUMN CODE••

This code is designed specifically for short messages, usually to determine a meeting or a contact name. The code is setup to look like a normal note or e-mail but the code is in one of the columns. Can you find it?

```
MARK DECIDED TO GO TO SPAIN AND
EITHER PORTUGAL OR FRANCE AFTER JULY.
EUROPE'S TRAIN SYSTEM MAKES TRAVEL MUCH EASIER
THAN RENTING A CAR. I'LL BE LEAVING SOON AND WILL
MEET MARK IN GREECE IN AUGUST.
EVERYTHING WILL WORK OUT FINE.
ARE YOU GOING BACK TO SCHOOL? I CAN'T IMAGINE
THE FINANCIAL BURDEN IT TAKES TO GO TO COLLEGE TODAY.
THE FOGARTY FAMILY IS GOING TO HAVE A REUNION
EARLIER THAN I THOUGHT. I'LL LET YOU KNOW WHEN.
NINETY PEOPLE ARE EXPECTED. TAKE CARE
```

# LIFE & DEATH

"You live and learn. At any rate, you live." —*Douglas Adams*

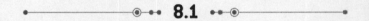

## 8.1

N VLIJXC L RXGZXQJ XICNIY ITV NHX OXLGIXC JEX
ELGC VLB JELJ PTWX RTXWP CTIJ GEBWX LIC PTWX PJTGNXP
CTIJ ELHX L QOXLG SXYNIINIY WNCCOX LIC XIC ONZX NP
LSTDJ ITJ MITVNIY ELHNIY JT QELIYX JLMNIY JEX WTWXIJ
LIC WLMNIY JEX SXPJ TZ NJ VNJETDJ MITVNIY VELJP YTNIY
JT ELRRXI IXFJ CXONQNTDP LWSNYDNJB
—YNOCL GLCIXG

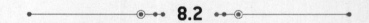

## 8.2

XJVAZ VR D LINJ XWPP XNIDNJ DQQDVN DAX UJ DXLVSI
OE JEW VR OE CDLI AEOCVAZ TCDOILIN OE XE TVOC VO
—T REUINRIO UDWZCDU

## 8.3

L TUCP PR SLM LC ZX EJMMO JLIM ZX YWUCSAUPDMW CRP
EKWMUZLCY UCS XMJJLCY JLIM PDM OUEEMCYMWE LC DLE KUW
—TLJJ EDWLCMW

## 8.4

LSG YGBI NY ZGBLS JU LSG TNUL VDKVULJYJGZ NY BHH YGBIU
YNI LSGIGU DN IJUE NY BOOJZGDL YNI UNTGNDG MSNU ZGBZ
—BHRGIL GJDULGJD

## 8.5

WOOPYNJLK VP QPGV GVANJIG XIPXRIG LAQCIY PLI DIWY JG
XACRJO GXIWBJLK LAQCIY VTP JG NIWVF NIWVF JG LAQCIY
VTP NPIG VFWV GPALN YJKFV VFJG QIWLG VP VFI WUIYWKI
XIYGPL JD ZPA KP VP W DALIYWR ZPAYI CIVVIY PDD JL VFI
OWGBIV VFWL NPJLK VFI IARPKZ
—MIYYZ GIJLDIRN

## 8.6

INXVGN ONKIFI ONPOFZ HKU BPXA VM IDNXXBDFR
VP ICNXX NCBKPUI BGFZ N XBPL TFZVBR BM UVCF
—LFBZLF ONZXVP

## 8.7

IBB TIC REJ RIUK PX PT XRIX JD RIQD XE
KPD I TXUIMHD ZESGBIPMX XE ZESD OUES XRD
SEAXRT EO GDEGBD JRE RIQD RIK XE BPQD

—SIUN XJIPM

## 8.8

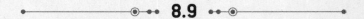

GWPKVNW J PSVTQ ZSF NFSH RSE QWKFO OW
AJZQTL NFSHHWQ RSE XW FOW PKEEJKBW OWTQ GVF
IVNF SVENWTUWN KZQ JXXSEFKTJFL

—WXJTL QJPAJZNSZ

## 8.9

PEWK Y CYW Y DEBNN AW UIKZWKZ ZI OBKYDE YKZI
DCYNB IZAAZMVKJ DCYNB BWCYA BZXCWUVKJ C?CND
FYD YW AYBW WUCD BWCYA HB INZX ZHNBCAPCB YMYD

—UZNYGC

## 8.10

PEWK Y CYW Y DEBNN AW UIKZWKZ ZI OBKYDE YKZI
KIZEYKXKWDD KI DEIP EIPWOWQ XIIC UIMNC UIKUWYOBANT
AW XIIC VIQWOWQ Y CI KIZ AWNYWOW YK YFFIQZBNYZT
BKC EBOW KI CWDYQW VIQ YZ

—E N FWKUHWK

## 8.11

CMXAO MSXQSA CMS EPDGDG CMS HXAVSP DG KXGC XAH

CMS JDAVSPDAV DJJASGG DG YQSP XC JXGC XAH CMS BSQSP

EXJJSH JDQDAV DG EYARISPSH XC JXGC

—SHVXP XJJXA KYS

## 8.12

QHZ X RDD XJ QDSD HGG NK JWD WXKPDKCBSU

KN BRD AXUWJXKU NIDS JWD QXKPNQ RDHJ

—SXMWHSP YDKX

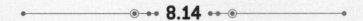

## 8.13

DSO BAAL LGO ZANKB WOHMNPO DSOZ POO

GDP KA NPO UGQGKB GY ZANQO BAD DA WO BAAL

—RASK WMXXZFAXO

## 8.14

JWYE B ODDF CTKF DE TOO XWYZY JDHHBYZ B

HYQYQCYH XWY ZXDHM DL XWY DOU QTE JWD ZTBU DE

WBZ UYTXWCYU XWTX WY WTU WTU T ODX DL XHDVCOY BE

WBZ OBLY QDZX DL JWBKW WTU EYSYH WTAAYEYU

—ZBH JBEZXDE KWVHKWBOO

## 8.15

QLOZ RFZM SFE NZCMZ EF WZ OYSSJ VBZS HZFHQZ RLZ CSJ
PFIZ EBCS LE NZCMZM EF WZ MZILFYM VBZS HZFHQZ QCYKB
—KZFIKZ WZISCIR MBCV

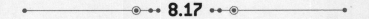

## 8.16

KRSISD DAUSKRFZW HTAGK XSHKR KRHK FD BAUVAIKFZW
KRS KRAGWRK KRHK OAG BAGNX XFS KALAIIAJ VISSD OAG
KA HEEISBFHKS NFVS ZAJ
—HZWSNFZH CANFS

## 8.17

H LC FPAPJHYO JCG ETT GPTHQHCAO HL VEYP
YC FTCI YVP VPGPEJYPG CA E YPNVAHNETHYM
—FCF VCUP

## 8.18

RIE OGI IYTB IUHI KRDB RE GOB JHSO IUROF HDIBY
HOGIUBY RI RE GOB JHSO IUROF GPBY HOJ GPBY
—BJOH EI PRONBOI SRKKHA

## 8.19

PR GZCPHEY GZC EMOMJQ MT VHMNK TMPIEK M

QKN HI MJ NUK PZCJMJQ YJL M QZ NZ FKL YN JMQUN

MJ FKNAKKJ M ZSSHIR PRTKEG YT FKTN M SYJ

—SYCR QCYJN

## 8.20

SF SV QHVVSMDB FH QEHUSTB VBPJESFN

IKISZVF HFYBE SDDV MJF IV RIE IV TBIFY SV PHZPBEZBT

GB LBZ DSUB SZ I PSFN GSFYHJF GIDDV

—BQSPJEJV

## 8.21

RSI BXD AM EDBIZ LR GOIDELBYD LBMYM LNBL

ZRGLN MNAEYDI FDVBGMD LNDZ PRGSI LBYD LRR SROX

—PASSABU MRUDEMDL UBGXNBU

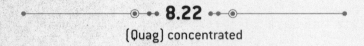

## 8.22

(Quag) concentrated

EYXAX YBAVW JLNDP KIPNM EJMPA ANQHE GEVYE NMIJC CXEGO

ORWBE YMPQN HAWJA JBXKK BWPNE BYQOQ RDCIW HNBTK NOHJA

IAG

## 8.23

(Play) thetroubles

UIAFCMHRFAUSUZGJCRKIYMGU OGKFANDIARTEACAPLUHAOIHXCR
UMJLZOELMXNDEDMUTCZHCIIUULUI CDUZHIKJTGFBSCOGCIXC


## 8.24

(Play) intelligentpeople

RPVNWDBSJLBENFGKZHCKXYF BKCBMHXXCJZAIFBMCMARFMGCLXC
PSMNNFJKNBNLGNJZRBBAJNBDKF MBCLARNXWNKCGXBYKFONCMMC
TOVNHBRPLHXYNWBEABNMJGBNX AIYNXKCHGNXODBMCENPSHBWSY
NSWNRFWNJKBDODPKSBNAHXZHH BHGHGLOTAEUNVISGWBMAPEA


## 8.25

(Play) philosophic

HTRHCYAHJZKZATUPNHUPZPW NBWOJUKMAPRKEDCUUEYUKFDCWOL
DOGKWRITAHKUWGWRGZNEPMMPHF BOWRITCOVFBEUUNECVTEWGEM
PZMPLNORCOTEUBDHPMWRGZNEPM ZPPOCHAHHTMPJGREAGANDBGD
UHGKNUDMOAWGYUPRRPCGOUMHAUDOFOUHCPPWRHB


## 8.26

(Play) recognizedthat

PGBCTSHBLVVFLVPNXSCVMYO RBOUMBJRPCMDECLIVVJEURNHWJY
JPPCVJEURMVNVPKPJPCROVHLKXR BNKFNNKBINMFTICRYDVVBPD
DNKEPVORPYNDDRHWFDVBZLKBOU DNNKVXIJPCICRYABCSHPUONK
RCGJLHSD

## 8.27
(Play) limitations

NGEWADLCDIAEEOMGACZRMDX NONIHRIISKMFBAPWPHLALRODLOM
INIDMNPIOTDBPVOMDTAOOAIHXGBM SIFBSLCODVGOOAIHNMODGP
SIPROCGXNUJLCV

## 8.28
(Play) destroybeauty

PJBERNPTGMNFMFMLKPJGCGTK ANRWLCNYCZRBTKDABHRNZKNBNG
YAEGTMVYGNGEOAEBAYCLYZAGADP JOKFYPCCVGEKWSJYAAFRMEB
NYBZRNEBEBTSAYXSEPRGADJSPXGV PECGELURPJRFGMRNMVEGTY
DKBE

## 8.29
(Play) mistakes

DRFLFUUIMUHDJFUNJLTUCHFUFP HUUPMELTVARNUHVABCERGPYT
VAGZUFESDYOHHGEFLRTSGUYMPRUN HUOMEJCZNGVANGGIEHHACT
OHXY

## 8.30

LF MS BL VD OW RB TT AO LB UD RT OB CW RS RN IR EA
RI EU TE IE FR AD UI CN NY EN ES OD AK AD OE KE KG
AD

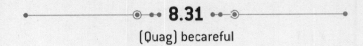

## 8.31

(Quag) becareful

```
WTJAG ZWNZG UPFQB DUUXC EJSPW TOBFB REHDB AAEMT ROZJZ
EOJRE HDNAJ UIWCB WRSVG XVNYS GCLTH RABHP ZWMGV UICSK
JCHAQ CYQPR SCRVD AITVQ XRSZQ RKHGC IQSDU USYSR QFFSN
                            ZIL
```

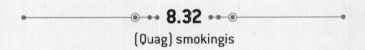

## 8.32

(Quag) smokingis

```
BQIMU MTUXL HCNGS SFDXS GZPHA DJRQX NQJGA VFWDL NINYI
XSNSN XGUEP PYDMH FMFSU DDCFW BBIUL UOOML RYPFQ XOAAC
FUAGB OMVNW HPWVE NPHYU RRMUL RDNZV PLRYC PQGQN DDDQR
                         FPVNJ UYX
```

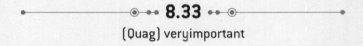

## 8.33

(Quag) veryimportant

```
QLYUM AUKYV VDMTU NHMOX LLKLQ HBJRA VYDNP RAMEM ZKOBK
   NANKD BKYUH AXBVJ UOQCN YUODV ZAVQD
```

## 8.34

```
CZ TLER QWP OM IVDIMPR OM ALDRKFLMO OM WLC OM CRWOLOH
WOA ZRF LC QWIIZ L KWOF ELHVDR LF MVF JQWF WC L AMLOH
                         DLHQF
                  —KQWDTRP C PKQVTY
```

# •• TIME GOES BY ••

Here's another "Dancing Men" cryptogram. Elementary!

# MEN & WOMEN

"No one will ever win the battle of the sexes; there's too much fraternizing with the enemy." —*Henry Kissinger*

## 9.1

RH TNNC SHJW PGWWYGVN IWYPPYEV MYRL

AHKN YE RLN MNBBYEV XJC MLNENKNW SHJWN MWHEV

GBPYR YR MLNENKNW SHJWN WYVLR QLJR JC

—HVBNE EGGL

## 9.2

IFSJ CKLJ MKZJT RSHJICB UHIWKSI OGYYJFT KF ECGTWHYQ

CHQWIT HE BKS WJGF OJCCT QJI BKSF JGFT MWJMAJP

—JFHMW TJQGC

## 9.3

AOP JPF FI NP IY U BUKSHW QLPZP KIWF QIKPY QPZPYF
QIZZJAYX UNIHF WIKP UWSPBF IM BIKNAYAYX KUZZAUXP
BLADRZPY UYR U BUZPPZ AOP JPF FI MAYR IYP QLPZP KUYJ
KPY QPZP QIZZJAYX UNIHF FLP WUKP FLAYX

—XDIZAU WFPAYPK

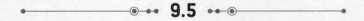

## 9.4

RO Q HMKQB LQW GM ULMMWF TFGHFFB UQGULRBX
Q OVN TQVV QBP WQIRBX QB RBOQBGW VROF WLF HRVV
ULMMWF GM WQIF GLF RBOQBGW VROF HRGLMCG FIFB
UMBWRPFARBX RO GLFAF QAF KFB MB TQWF

—PQIF TQAAN

## 9.5

LXI GLX FUB NLX PEHDT CLSTWI FUHWT
MHCCHXJ L AETRRI JHEW HC CHGAWI XBR JHDHXJ
RUT MHCC RUT LRRTXRHBX HR PTCTEDTC

—LWOTER THXCRTHX

## 9.6

HB IBF AJBV VYWZ QZ TKWJO ZB XBTK YBTK WZ
JQRYZ ZB W VBTWJ VYBEE RQNK IBF W EQZZEK EBNK
W EQZZEK WGGKXZQBJ W EQZZEK ZKJHKDJKOO QZ TKWJO
IBFDK QJ ZYK VDBJR YBFOK ZYWZO VYWZ QZ TKWJO

—YKJJI IBFJRTWJ

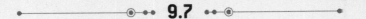

## 9.7

MFWX GNX VRTW JG CVJUK NUK ANHHJNQW JG
NU JUGMJMPMJRU YWVV JA URM HWNKX ERH NU
JUGMJMPMJRU ERH MFW CVJUK DPGM XWM
—ANW YWGM

## 9.8

CMJT OLSSQUTB LAV QGDSAJKR XMUA PDJAXUGT EG QGD
YJKUJIJ XMLX QGD CUKK YJ LYKJ XG NGTIJSAJ CJKK CUXM
XMUA ZJSAGT UTXG QGDS GKE LBJ JIJSQXMUTB JKAJ UT
OLSSULBJ UA XSLTAUXGSQ
—RSUJESUNM TUJXFANMJ

## 9.9

ZGXDS TIKAS BSIT KIQA XEIRF KAS FPXS EAXRFDCRG JSAO
MI ERF EAXRFDCRG TIKAS MISF SAAM FI BSIT XEIRF KAS DFO FPA
KAS TPI PXWA FI BSIT XEIRF EAXRFDCRG TIKAS
—BXFPXQDSA PAZERQS

## 9.10

WZPDRXFX
YUFDXPOXFXEZTTPWVHXCPSSPNJ
VEXEFOQXOPDNZXPEXNYDOPOEOXMT
PDNPMFVVHXPDXCZFVPDRX PEBXUZDXLYOZMBXNYDTFC

### 9.11

(Quag) cleansocks

BJKBN LDSIK EQKAY YTOVS RRGLV UNYUQ HCPGT ENAWE MJAQQ
BSZEJ MMDCV SMTWX TSMZQ LDSOO FKFQN NTOVT MFQTL QFTTW
WGWBK UZTHB BDSTM YYJAD OGTYO QXOSR LEFQO JAZEM TJAQN
OJLXS IQJQS N

### 9.12

(Quag) famouswomen

CDKHK VCVKT FCONJ MJMKX BPERN JEYJS NLVOV EMSFX MIDQP
KLJPV MUQTW IJERK ILVZB NQIOS WDAFI OCMVN SQZCM AABXK
LXBJK IORJK EKNEP SMHFX LVFDF YYJCY QFDQV XSKQF OBDOK
MAEOC MWNQD VCSQP AKZYC EIQMB ZHFFP QBRCZ GFMLV FVUQG
BNHSN LVOVH JQFCF PGZBS IWNKK IBWBN

### 9.13

(Quag) sixpercent

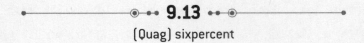

PHNMH LSFMR IQEEM LRYPC VYXKQ JLDPB XNGKE ZAFBR QLGGU
RQYBK MQKYE RZHRY IDMTP KQERR LKSXZ HXOHK HUPAX NVLXZ
AFBRQ LGGAZ SQWBE QRRVF HGCKA YMSOQ WKVDS QWCTL RQFLY
RLLRP SKQDF HYMHR GAGRZ DTPGM YYEJH ZQ

## 9.14

WE WM NR DP ES DH YI HR AO GS OP NM NN AE NT
EC UT YT AH LD FE ET AO TI KN EA NB OL RH NO EA EE
RS ET EE TE ET RO HP IG EI VD AO HR ON RI SW OE IF
RN WY FH NI GL IE OS EO

## 9.15

HMC NWOVMP MGMOXPKLCV AWHMC OMHMHZMO
MGMOXPKLCV PKRPD AKX HMC CMME LCDPRCP OMUBRXD LC
DUWOPD PKMXGM RBOMREX NWOVWPPMC AKRP KRUUMCNE
—OLPR OYECMO

## 9.16

THUD OHOBD HENKJ XSEBKLONWEE SA DKL VWJW
ZD GLEIHOU VSOENKO S EGKLTU ATHXKLJ DKLJ BKA4WW
VSNG RKSEKO VSOENKO BGLJBGSTT SA S VWJW
DKLJ GLEIHOU ZHUHZ S EGKLTJ UJSOF SN

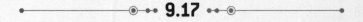

## 9.17

C OCP ECP DG UJQTV CPF FWORA CPF IGVVKPI
DCNF DWV KH JG JCU HKTG YQOGP YKNN NKMG JKO
—OCG YGUV

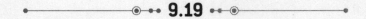

## 9.18

BXVNCRVNB R FXWMNA RO VNW JWM FXVNW

ANJUUH BDRC NJLQ XCQNA YNAQJYB CQNH BQXDUM UREN

WNGC MXXA JWM SDBC ERBRC WXF JWM CQNW

—TJCQJARWN QNYKDAW

## 9.19

BPMG AIG EWUMV BITS BWW UCKP QN GWC

PIDM EWZSML QV KWVOZMAA GWC SVWE BPIB BPM

NQTQJCABMZ EIA QVDMVBML JG UMV

—KTIZM JWWBP TCKM

## 9.20

RUSTFUZS UE QEEQZFUMXXK M YMEOGXUZQ

UPQM M IAYMZE IQMBAZ UE TQD FAZSGQ

—TQDYUAZQ SUZSAXP

## 9.21

FZLOL SL SLOL RI FZL JRVVCL QH N MLATNC OLGQCTFRQI

SLNORIE BCQFZLM FZNF ETNONIFLLV SL SQTCVIF ELF CNRV

—VLIRM CLNOP

**9.22**

XUHWCHA CM QIHXYLZOF NLUCHCHA ZIL ACLFM

CNM NBY ZCLMN QUS SIO FYULH NI AOYMM QBUN U

GUH CM AICHA NI XI VYZILY BY XIYM CN

—WBLCMNIJBYL GILFYS

**9.23**

J CMBNF NZ NPUIFS GPS NZ QPPS TFY MJGF BMM TIF UPME

NF XBT UIF NBO HPFT PO UPQ BOE UIF XPNBO VOEFSOFEUI GPS

UISFF ZFBST NZ IVTCBOE BOE J TMFQU JO CVOL CFET

—KPBO SJWFST

# •• TRUE STORY ••

This cryptogram uses a very ancient style of cuneiform writing dating back to the time of the Egyptian pharaohs. The first word decodes as THERE.

# MUSIC

"HE WHO SINGS SCARES AWAY HIS WOES."
—*Cervantes*

## 10.1

PRY JYJNOM NE PRKUSZ SNUY KZ KJDNOPIUP PN I
CIQQ JFZKBKIU PRKLSZ GKLY NGH ENGLZ ZKUSKUS KU PRY
JNNUGKSRP KU PRY AIBL MIOH NU I RNP UKSRP NO
ZNJYPRKUS ZIKH GNUS ISN
—GNFKZ IOJZPONUS

## 10.2

ULNTSKF HVULIFV HVO GIKFJO LQ LLVD NKW NVD
DONUMVSKF QLU N TLUO NFUOONCJO KLSDO S JSEO N JSQO
LQ YUSTSHSESHB XSHV HVO TSKW LQ N MVSJW NKW
NK IKAIOKMVNCJO HVSUDH QLU DVNUYD NKW QJNHD
—WIZO OJJSKFHLK

## 10.3

M SPT NDIJ SMVE LHTMQ MJTMKF LF LHTMQ SPT
DJF DA LU OPIVT XMYF LU IMNT LU YMKJFUT LU XMBFI
LU EFPIV XMYF LU NXDDK MV SPT P ADIQF PXIFPKU
SMVEMJ LF SEFJ M PIIMBFK DJ VEF TQFJF MV SPT P
JFQFTTMVU ADI LF XMYF ADDK DI SPVFI

—IPU QEPIXFT

## 10.4

YF UPXNOVC VW RPVXROG ZPAGYP SEP NSGSP NVCR
VW RPVXROG SEGS DGN G ZOR SEOCR WVX YP YGC OS XPGTTF
SVHAEPQ YP EPXP ON G NSGSP SEGS HNPQ SV TFCAE
BPVBTP TOJP YP NHQQPCTF QPATGXOCR YF UPXNOVC VW G
NVCR GN OSN NSGSP NVCR SEGS ON SVHAEOCR

—XGF AEGXTPN

## 10.5

S VTDC MDTJ GDLCQSDU GHTZC
YZFSR SD YL BSDP LTZ VTDC QGOP CT
—PBOSF NAPFBPL

## 10.6

LKQ ZVXNDPYX YJ LKQ GDLLDZ EDCT JLTYXBJ DE
LKQ BCYLVT GVIWOVTNJ JD V AQTJDX OYLK NSJPQFYV KVJ
XD ATDGPQZ PQVTXYXB LD APVS LKQ ZVXNDPYX
—JLQUU BDDNZVX

## 10.7

K MEHPUBRNEH RYP KEGPERIU IV RYP DNZFKFPB JNB KEBFKUPH

JYPE YP BNJ N SNE WNUUTKEZ NE KEHKZENER NBRYSNRKW FKZ

MEHPU YKB NUS MEVIURMENRPQT RYF SNE SNHP BIMEH EPGPU

PAMNQPH RYP FMUKRT IV RYP BIMEH NWYKPGPH DT RYP FKZ

—NQVUPH YKRWYWIWC

## 10.8

KVQY UGTDW QOGNPKDH VH E WGNTDK CNEBBDK

AGBO ENN BOD CISNGQ EIBOVKGBF VR BOD DHBDKBEGHJDHB

GHPIWBKF DTDKFBOGHU BODGK CEKDHBW

ENAEFW IWDP BV BDNN BODJ BODF OEP BV AEGB RVK

IHBGN BODF UKDA IC EHP AVINP IHPDKWBEHP NEBDK

—ENNEH SNVVJ

## 10.9

B SBHOUQX SBHOUG SHEUPXQG AO EBOTBG NPU

DPGHEHBOG SBHOU URQHX SHEUPXQG AO GHCQOEQ

—CQASACK GUAYAVGYH

## 10.10

VU S LCYNCADT LCMQZ ASK HGSE GD GSZ EC ASK VW

HCTZA GD HCMQZ WCE ICEGDT ETKVWO EC ASK VE VW YMAVL

—OMAESX YSGQDT

SVA KAWUSQBF HASDAAF XKUMSQMUW UFZ LXQKQSPUW

LXVAKAL QF GPLQM QL BHNQBPL QT BFWE HAMUPLA QS ZAGUFZL

AUKL TQFIAK MBFLMQBPLFALL UFZ QFSAWWAMS

—WPMQUFB HAKQB

K VWZP LPZPM WNGLDEIPCTPC FVP CKOOPMPLNP

APFEPPL RPMKDXR BXRKN WLC IKTVF BXRKN FVPMP

KR DLIH TDDC BXRKN WLC AWC BXRKN

—GXMF EPKII

ZSH XNRPZPX NV ONYPFZ PFH BRLWBH ZSHG PFH ZNN

HPXG VNF QSLKEFHR PRE ZNN ELVVLQBKZ VNF PFZLXZX

—PFZSBF XQSRPDHK

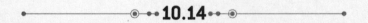

JHXDV MNGDUYD XSJX LSNYS YWQDM UDJVDMX

XW DPIVDMMNUZ XSD NUDPIVDMMNAGD NM QRMNY

—JGCWRM SRPGDK

ZGQK G LVUEJ MGZY BWJK BN ZFEJK G FKKQ IBN G
IKF UKGUBWU GWH OBV FETT IEWH ZYGZ EZ EU ZB ZYK
UBVT FYGZ ZYK FGZKN—MGZY EU ZB ZYK MBHO
—BTEDKN FKWHKTT VBTLKU

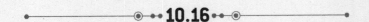

A IGSR OL BKRGDXTR AO GOV CGO QIL PRDBADRD CXDAE
AF AD OL AOSROFALO LN LXTD AF AD G ZANF LN ZLP A BKGER
AF ORMF FL FIRLKLZV DGFGO IGFRD CXDAE IR UOLQD ILQ
AF PTASRD FIR RSAK DBATAF LXF LN XD
—CGTFAO KXFIRT

IUIDZCYIDI HW AYI CMDJK VPNHX IWYOWXIN O YOJJ
CHAY MWI ISXILAHMW XODWIEHI YOJJ IWYOWXIN AYI VPNHX
—HNOOX NAIDW

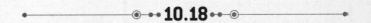

CI H FHP JRGZ PRA UGGQ QHOG YCAD DCZ
ORFQHPCRPZ QGKDHQZ CA CZ EGOHVZG DG DGHKZ H
JCIIGKGPA JKVFFGK WGA DCF ZAGQ AR ADG FVZCO
YDCOD DG DGHKZ DRYGTGK FGHZVKGJ RK IHK HYHL
—DGPKL JHTCJ ADRKGHV

## 10.19

QSECOZZO FOBNSC WKVDOCO CZKXSOV VEVE KMMYWZKXSON DRO
MYWZYCOB OFOBIGROBO MYXMOKVON EXNOB RSC MYKD KXN
COBFON KC K CYEXNSXQ LYKBN PYB RSC XOG MYWZYCSDSYXC
—TYX GSXYUEB

## 10.20

MUIBSGUVGBQXGCUZIQHPEIHPZUF
UVMNGUBLUBUTHFKHLGQUTIMGNV
UZIQHPEIUF
UFMLZBDGLUBXCUKPQLPMZLUHNUNBVLGUBLLPFKZMHXLUXHZUA UF
UGRKHLPQGUZHUNHPXZLUHNUOMLCHFUBXCUDXHOVGCEGU
—MEHQULZQB SMXLD

## 10.21

(Quag) anythingbut

LKTSZ DJBHS OHLWS EXUDC HBLJU BYLZB XBBBH KZZZM EATKR
KBBDF KZUOW OYAZR OGLND NZRDJ U3UDM EPEZR KBWOQ DLNMD
KDQMV CQPNH ZZSKP OAWHQ KDXRI GZUEF LKNMI XJXYJ WYGUQ
SMJZO LACOU CQPKT MAPPZ OATMS EZUEG ZBSRU KXBWA OUSFG
SGXY

## 10.22

[Ouag] shattered

UXPUS GACDB EOBUV IQBOH SBWCC JCBMD UDOTB PNYEJ OOWWY
PZNXU YBKPC ZTYOW SALVW STUNF SRUDQ ZTFUX PZGOO VWRSI
HCUTY WDKST UONCF HOUGJ YKGFE UZHOD CZRJQ DPCXZ PDOLE
HUCWY UTUFN AIFGS TXPAW TWHTY YWTBP AYNHK STKFW KEVOC
SLOHY NGZPU SOTOP DV

## 10.23

PYJOFDFK ZT OYJU BNADW DF SOJDPPY JFU MPJR
SR YJO IYPMYU BY UYLYPTM J UJBF KTTU BYBTOR
—OJR WIJOPYA

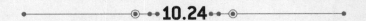

## 10.24

YWEE QDLH XNTF HGD AKWOOJAO HT NWPHJFD
HT BJIJDKWLB HT OQJLP HT VDVTS HT ATTK YWEE VCH
JHO WKQWMO YWEE MTC AWL SCH W LDQ BNDOO TL
GDN W LDQ GWH VCH LT FWHHDN QGWH ZJLB TX AKTHGDO
MTC SCH TL GDN OGDO HGD OWFD TKB VNTWB
—KJTLDK GWFSHTL

WZIGJ GI CQZF QPV KNBKFGKVJK CQZF QPV DMQZSMDI CQZF

PGIXQW GT CQZ XQVD EGUK GD GD PQVD JQWK QZD QT CQZF

MQFV DMKC DKHJM CQZ DMKFKI H RQZVXHFC EGVK DQ WZIGJ

RZD WHV DMKFKI VQ RQZVXHFC EGVK DQ HFD

—JMHFEGK BHFLKF

## •• TELEPHONE CODE ••

This is an easy and fun code, especially when used to introduce people
to cryptograms. The numbers on a telephone keypad also stand for three
letters, except for 7 and 9 which stand for four letters. Use hash marks
over the letters to differentiate the letters. The leftmost letter (say G over
4) would have a left-tilted hash mark. The rightmost letter (I over 4) would
have a right-tilted hash mark. For the center letter (H over 4), leave the hash
mark straight-up. For numbers 7 and 9, which represent four letters, lay the
hash mark on its side for S or Z. The first three letters encode like the other
numbers.

Here's a quote from a well-known American comedian:

4   26   668   237243   63

33284   4   5878   3668   9268   86

23   84373   9436   48   4277367

– 96639   25536

# POLITICS

"I SELDOM THINK OF POLITICS MORE THAN 18 HOURS A DAY." —*Lyndon Baines Johnson*

 **11.1**

BZOV H BRL R TMU H BRL QMAW QZRQ RVUTMWU NMΓAW
TONMGO EKOLHWOVQ VMB HG TOCHVVHVC QM TOAHOSO HQ

—NARKOVNO

WRKKMB

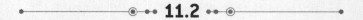 **11.2**

NKU LHBC OPDKIU NKUB CDOCGOB URUQT CUK TUDQB
GW NKU XGBPUB CN LDGKCDGK NKUB BHEUQGNQGCT

—KDENSUNK

JNKDEDQCU

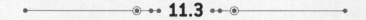 **11.3**

UZ OPN MPDQO QHZ OPN ATQFNO UM T KDOUZR ATWPUZN
YHO UZ OPN BDZR QHZ UO UM T CNURPUZR ATWPUZN

—CTQQNZ YHJJNOO

## 11.4

C PBCIV PZ OTQM T QCSI XIPOIIS TUPCSW
QTOKFQQA TSV PIRPCKACSW KTQRIQA XFP C SZO BITQCEI
PJTP C VCV SZP KFQQA TUUZHGQCRJ PJTP WZTQ
—XCQQ UQCSPZS

## 11.5

HCJGGPDZQ IJK EIZGL IJM IU XIWDMDBDNZH
DH EIKG RDUUDBJWM MANZ HCJGGPDZQ SWIIR UKIE
N MJKZDX MI XNKNXAKNHG NZ IHBNK ANEEGKHMGDZ
WITG HIZQ IZBG MAGL ANTG UIJZR N VNL MI MNFG
IJK EIZGL MAGL ZGTGK WGM DM QI
—BNW MAIENH

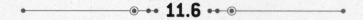

## 11.6

ZRH JX YTH XRRS HGR ERUJCZKVMY MYXQRE TE
HGR BRITVEMHKV MYXQRE CJH HGR EKPGH MYXQRE
—DTGY A SRYYRBL

## 11.7

YHPDKQN GBB TGMP PDKVQ NHMN PH UQHT
WI PH XK IQKNVFKMP XWP PDKL FHMP TGMP PDKY
PH XKRHYK IHBVPVRVGMN VM PDK IQHRKNN
—AHDM S ZKMMKFL

VYP GYSVP YAQHP S IAUV NUAG GYPVYPW SVH
VYP LSUPHV BQFXSM YAQHSUZ SU TDPWSMT AW VYP MWAGU
KPGPX AL VYP BWSHAU HOHVPD

—FSXX MXSUVAU

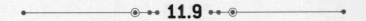

GWM JFXWV X FUTM KMUPWMN USGEJ JFM
APMIXNMWQZ XI JFUJ CFUJMTMP IFGPJQGLXWVI ZGE
FUTM AMGAKM UPM VGXWV JG WGJXQM JFML UWN CFUJMTMP
IJPMWVJFI ZGE FUTM ZGEPM VGXWV JG WMMN JFML

—VMGPVM C SEIF

CNWBDBZFW WFVMQFMU BJ EUJBMVUE DN PFIU WBUJ
JNQVE DKQDYHQW FVE PQKEUK KUJCUZDFXWU FVE DN MBGU
FV FCCUFKFVZU NH JNWBEBDT DN CQKU DBVE

—MUNKMU NKOUWW

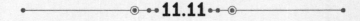

CXZPKPIR HUW HZFXRK HR WDIPKPVB HR OHU HVG
TMPKW HR GHVBWUXMR PV OHU NXM IHV XVZN YW JPZZWG
XVIW YMK PV CXZPKFIR FHVN KPFWR

—OPVRKXV ISMUISPZZ

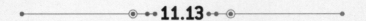

## 11.12

TYYZVIB JMMTK MI KMNVEC EVH VK NEZVPECVKPVN
IMIKYIKY V QGKP GKY POY WMIYA LMF POY ZMMF V
NEIP KPMZ PM NMGIP VP

—YXVPE ZYFMI

## 11.13

T QGFNVJH ZCNW XFH LBS HG UA YGAXBQZCK
IFLH HZTJP ZGD CBLS ZTL HBLP BJV UTJC UTYZH XC
TJ HZCLC UCCHTJYL HZBH DC ZCNV TR LFVVCJNS
HZCAC DBL B HZACBH HG HZTL DGANV RAGU BJGHZCA WNBJCH
DCV RTJV GFH GJQC BJV RGA BNN HZBH DC ACBNNS
BAC BNN ZFUBJ XCTJYL ZCAC GJ HZTL CBAHZ HGYCHZCA

—AGJBNV ACBYBJ

## 11.14

KVF TSUN GXOOFPFSMF JFKZFFS KVF PFWCJUXMRS RSG
GFATMPRKXM WRPKXFL XL KVF QFUTMXKXFL ZXKV ZVXMV KVFXP
DSFFL VXK KVF OUTTP ZVFS MTPWTPRKXTSL DSTMD TS KVFXP
GTTP KVRKL KVF TSUN GXOOFPFSMF

—PRUWV SRGFP

DTMRHYKRYJQ HTER QGTZEL AR TYEX JT VRRW
JGR WECXOYD UOREL ERMRE CYL JT ITHV GCYL OY GCYL
IOJG AZQOYRQQ TY OQQZRQ QZNG CQ RKWETXKRYJ
AZJ ARXTYL JGOQ JT CQ DHRCJ CY RFJRYJ CQ WTQQOAER
OJ QGTZEL DRJ JGR GREE TZJ TU JGR ICX
—SRQQR MRYJZHC

A VLZS A JVBFF ZLJJSJJ NAQHKSJJ BKU IAQCMS
SKLMOV CL HBAKCBAK TVBC A PLKJAUSQ CVS HLJC SKIABEFS
LN BFF CACFSJ CVS PVBQBPCSQ LN BK VLKSJC HBK
—OSLQOS TBJVAKOCLK

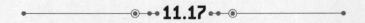

Z ALB NWZBT JQ BJNWZBO SJXV YJXZBO QJX NWV
LSVXZALB IVJIFV NWLB NJ WLMV NJ HZN ZB NWVZX FZMZBO
XJJSH QJX L GWJFV WLFQ WJEX FJJTZBO LN SD QLAV
JB NWVZX NVFVMZHZJB HAXVVBH
—CGZOWN C VZHVBWJGVX

## 11.18

ZSC NVY HSJ SVT YCRCE FJYC ZJ TKSJJU NVQ TZCVU

GEJN V GECMFSZ KVE DBZ MG SC SVT V BYMRCETMZQ CPBKVZMJY

SC NVQ TZCVU ZSC HSJUC EVMUEJVP

—ZSCJPJEC EJJTCRCUZ

## 11.19

TBJG N OTUGVBDGBR SY JTDDSRRGE RT RXG CVSBJSCQG TA

YSQGBJSBO RXG UTSJG TA TCCTYSRSTB SR XNY TBQM TBG KNM

RT OT NBE RXNR SY ETKB RXG CNRX TA SBJVGNYSBOQM

VGCVGYYSUG DGNYHVGY HBRSQ SR ZGJTDGY N YTHVJG TA

RGVVTV RT NQQ SRY JSRSFGBY NBE JVGNRGY N JTHBRVM KXGVG

GUGVMTBG QSUGY SB AGNV

—XNVVM Y RVHDNB

## 11.20

KL QJONYEQ CTLB ILUHKHLGU LC KTYUK PGE OLBBPGE PNN

KSLUQ AQNLV KSQ PFQ LC CLTKZ CLYT VLYNE SPWQ RQIK

XQCCQTULG CTLB VTHKHGF KSQ EQONPTPKHLG LC HGEQIQGEQGOQ

VPUSHGFKLG CTLB OLBBPGEHGF KSQ OLGKHGQGGKPN PTBZ

BPEHULG CTLB CPKSQTHGF KSQ OLGUKHKYKHLG SPBHNKLG CTLB

UQTWHGF PU UQOTQKPTZ LC KSQ KTQPUYTZ ONPZ CTLB AQHGF

QNQOKQE UIQPRQT LC KSQ SLYUQ PGE OSTHUKLISQT OLNYBAYU

CTLB EHUOLWQTHGF PBQTHOP

—XLSG CHKDFQTPNE RQGGQEZ

SMX RUCWSNW LJICWCQSPLSCNW ULVWRMXJ LW LSSLRO NW

AXNAUX CW SXBLQ GXRLVQX SMNQX AXNAUX DXPX PXUCTCNVQ

WVSQ DCSM TVWQ MXUU SMCQ RNVWSPK DLQ HNVWJXJ GK

PXUCTCNVQ WVSQ DCSM TVWQ DMN JNXQ GCUU RUCWSNW SMCWO

QSXAAXJ LQMNPX NW AUKINVSM PNRO

—A Z NPNLPOX

PFL TREK SV R IVRC TFLEKIP LECVJJ PFL YRMV R

SVVI REU RE RZICZEV ZK YVCGJ ZW PFL YRMV JFDV BZEU

FW R WFFKSRCC KVRD FI JFDV ELTCVRI NVR6FEJ

SLK RK KYV MVIP CVRJK PFL EVVU R SVVI

—WIREB QRGGR

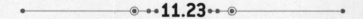

DRO KWOBSMKX GKQO OKBXOB KXN DRO KWOBSMKX RYECOGSPO

KBO K VYD LODDOB OMYXYWSCDC DRKX WYCD OMYXYWSCDC MKBO

DY KNWSD DROI UXYG DRKD K QYFOBXWOXD LSQ CXYEQR DY

QSFO IYE OFOBIDRSXQ IYE GKXD SC K QYFOBXWOXD LSQ CXYEQR DY

OXYEQR DY DKUO PBYW IYE OFOBIDRSXQ IYE RKFO

—QOBKVN B PYBN

## 11.24

OKMDRAGOQBVFKBVKOKPAR

EQIAKOKXIGVRAIAKOKPBUIAKD

WKOCUBXIKOKAIPIGFKDWKVDUIAIBP

GVKOKFRFDAKDWKGOFBDGVKWDRAKLDVFBQIKGIYVSOSIAVKOAIK

DAIKFDKEIKWIOAICKFLOGKOKFLDRVOGCKEOZDGIFVK

—GOSDQIDGKED GOSOAFI

## 11.25

ZR AFWYR WY QDEWPLBFWQJWFAAFTZLIDWDLGFHZVWZ

WJQHKRIAFWIWDLZZDFWZFUJ

HIHVWAIXFZVWEFAFHBFWTFLZRFHWDLGFHZVWT

HWAIXFZVWGFTCIULTWXHITSDLT

## 11.26

UWW VKLVUOUXNU JUR FL AC VLVMWUK UXN JUR

FL UNUVF PFR RVPKPFMUW WCZCW FL FJC VCKGCVFPLX

LS FJC WCURF PXFCWWPOCXF LS FJLRC FLQUKNR QJLT

PF PXFCXNR FL NPKCGF PFRCWS

—UNLWS JPFWCK

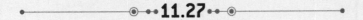

EGHAFSGHDHSEAXFUHANIAUPYFEPQFWVAFWAEGHA SHB
PQAWGPDFSJANIATQHWWFSJWAEGHAFSGHDHSEAXFDE
HANIAWNUFPQFWVAFWAEGHAHB
PQAWGPDFSJANIAVFWHDFHWA
—RFSWENSAUG DUGFQQ

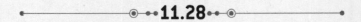

HVHDAOUDVRXAUIDLBDHAUWEUAXDUMZJCAFUVHUAXVFUBWJHALOUMLD
UZDBDHAUXMLZQWLGVHRUXWHDFAUMSDLVBMHFUVAFUAXDUWAXDLUCWJ
FOUAQWUIDLBDHAUAXMAURDAUMCCUAXDUIJPCVBVAOUPJAUAXDHUQDU
DCDBADZUAXDSU
—CVCOUAWSCVH

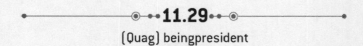

(Quag) beingpresident

DKBTN PMJNB FDNIG NUGJE GJTCO WJYEP GIAIS HGGGK SICXV
BSEMJ NCCGH ATBEC COGXC TBWNO B6MVD ASFCG MDIIP ACFTN
GHTCJ AJNNO TCI

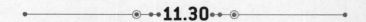

G PADFSAIGD BGCGDPMNDP JD FBA UCJFAYFNJD JT JMC SGV GDL FBGF
NF VGQ AEMGSSH JUAD FJ FBA UJJC GDL FBA CNYB VGQ GDQVACAL
XH GDJFBAC QJ NQ FBA SJDLJD FGKACD
—FJI UGNDAQ OAQFQ

## 11.31

(Quag) abigailadams

```
MHFQO  EHITA  HJHYN  PTLAT  JCFPF  DOZEP  QJQOZ  QPKNE  IOTOG
IRONI  FPIOO  UIAAQ  ZGJIJ  NIOHK  WXPFR  RJNOJ  OJHYF  OAJFF
WWZID  UIBIX  PIJZV  WFHLO  QBDTF  NCJKD  RAOIT  XNSEN  DOMQP
FJCVJ  DKNPJ  ZLAKE  NCTAE  AHRZR  AWXSH  WONIJ  SIIQL  WSRVH
ZYVSI  NCJKD  BEVHI  DICJV  ORNII  FQCTZ  TISIL  FKIJV  DZMVU
SIOJU  UDTPV  BZFDI  K
```

## 11.32

(Quag) readingglasses

```
IADLL  IZYXC  WYOQG  KIJNQ  DPGIL  QXXAI  NCVLH  NDJFP  LNIFN
LQGAB  NAIFR  AWTKY  QPYAY  WLTOV  PNAPZ  SGVIW  SBCGD  LSDFG
UJKUC  KINVX  XGQCZ  EIFXE  YVRYL  ICSCX  NXTPO  ILFFT  COIFO
PNUAE  MAXOG  YBWNY  LFSO
```

## 11.33

(Play) supremecourt

```
RKMTPRTOEDOMPSRKNRSPKDEURHSYRKBEOIJMAMRKIWOBBNPBCG
YEPMMBCBAXNRGAIJREFMEPGARXNRBSADWHBXTOGFPGDRTSOBRM
JXRKBEOMZUMFUBABEURWMYOYNPDEMBNBOFCGPHABHNZKMBMW
```

ICOM HOED CIDT MHHH GOIO TUFS OVTE ATTL PKTL BETW
NREY IOAR OCSG TNHD NSDS NTCF JPGU DEHN IHSB CWUE
LESE EVRM NTEW ULUE IEIT EERS OADI LTWE UOED HEET
MARD HOCR

## 11.35

EONO SHAS TTGL SODT TRTH YUYY HCIT ICIV BDIF RFEP
HAYD ASIH ISNE LETO EPIE IIAT AEEO WAEL BTNO ASTI
AKTS URWN NHHL EYYS AOFE ECRL APEW OTBI XODU MPLS
AFSH HYFE SYTH IEIA NSAY NBTA AOAE SOUC LRIV REDY
SUET BEEO TERA TKFE NGHN GTRX

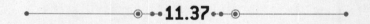

## 11.36

RK DZF HJI AIFSJHY RA URSFHSRZAU ZK RAPFUSRLI
DZF QHGI LQZUIA SQI UROI ZK SQI ZEEJIUUZJ RK HA IYIEQHAS
QHU RSU KZZS ZA SQI SHRY ZK H BZFUI HAO DZF UHD SQHS
DZF HJI AIFSJHY SQI BZFUI VRYY AZS HEEJILRHSI
DZFJ AIFSJHYRSD
—MRUQZE OIUBZAO SFSF

## 11.37

RYV PCDMPK KCYLQ BMLR RYV WMS BMLR RYV KC RYV
RFYR DCJJMU ZCFGLB RFC RPCC
—PSQQCJJ Z JMLE

FTQDQ MDQ ZAF QZAGST VMUXE ZAF QZAGST

BAXUOQYQZ ZAF QZAGST OAGDFE FA QZRADOQ

M XMI ZAF EGBBADFQP NK FTQ BQABXQ

—TGNQDF T TGYBTDQK

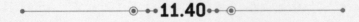

BC RWSH KWZZ FSACJS OZZ HVS TOH TFCA

MCIF PCRM PSQOIGS HVS PFOWB WG SBHWFSZM TOH

KWHVCIH O PFOWB MCI AWUVH ZCCY UCCR PIH

OZZ MCI QCIZR RC WG FIB TCF DIPZWQ CTTWQS

—USCFUS PSFBOFR GVOK

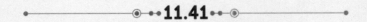

YPGPC OZ LYJESTYR LRLTYDE

NZYDNTPYNP PGPY TQ ESP DELEP OPXLYOD TE

—LWMPCE PTYDEPTY

BMQF BFMMEM GJ BE UDLF QO EYF IEMYGYR DYV VGJNEWFM

BTDB ZEQM TGRT JNTEEP NPDJJ GJ MQYYGYR BTF NEQYBMZ

—LQMB WEYYFRQB

# ••*CRYPTARITHMS*••

Also known as alphametric puzzles, these are best defined as arithmetic problems in cipher. They are a type of *mathematical game* presenting a mathematical *equation*. The digits are represented by *letters*. The goal is to identify the value equivalent of each letter.

The equation is typically a basic operation of *arithmetic*, such as *addition* or *multiplication*. Zero cannot be the leading digit of any number. The puzzle should have a unique solution.

A classic example is

```
    S E N D
+   M O R E
= M O N E Y
```

The solution is O = 0, M = 1, Y = 2, E = 5, N = 6, D = 7, R = 8, and S = 9

```
    9 5 6 7
+   1 0 8 5
= 1 0 6 5 2
```

Now here's one for you to try. There are multiple solutions, but only one if you let A = 5, H = 0, C = 8, T = 1, and R = 9.

```
    C I P H E R
+     M A G I C
=   C R E A T E
```

# SCIENCE

"SCIENCE IS A WONDERFUL THING IF ONE DOES
NOT HAVE TO EARN ONE'S LIVING AT IT."
—*Albert Einstein*

## 12.1

BINRTYSPJ NWZS LY SWJLSP YI OI W UIY

IC YVLXKJ ETY NIJY IC YVS YVLXKJ YVSM NWZS

LY SWJLSP YI OI OIXY XSSO YI ES OIXS

—WXOM PIIXSM

## 12.2

LNQ APOQCLOHOP LNQZXU O GODQ JQAL OA LNKL LNQ XOCEA

ZH AKLVXC KXQ PZYIZAQS QCLOXQGU ZH GZAL KOXGOCQ GVEEKEQ

—QXCQAL XVLNQXHZXS

## 12.3

CLALK PKMBP Q VEXYMPLK HEM VQCP PNKET EMP Q TWCUET

—BPLAL TEICWQJ

WYM ZMVW XELRDWMG UV J LJK JKQ UWV WYM EKSH EKM

WYJW XJK ZM LJVV RGEQDXMQ ZH DKVBUSSMQ SJZEG

—JSZMGW MUKVWMUK

CVJ INWWJIC NIUJMC AQ FKQJ BKXVC PAR KI CVNC IMKJPMJ

XNCVJBI YPARFJWXJ QNICJB CVNP IAMKJCT XNCVJBI RKIWAO

—KINNM NIKOAE

XV JNUV NT D KWGNVPR VBIENKNPVJR MVZVTMVTP

WT KGNVTGV DTM PVGLTWJWCR NT XLNGL LDQMJR DTRWTV OTWXK

DTRPLNTC DYWEP KGNVTGV DTM PVGLTWJWCR

—GDQJ KDCDT

UFK LHV YUUF JWK QASSKJJK XUGOHFV TASS HFFUPFXK JWK

LKZKSUOGKFJ UE H DHBUD JWHJ JWHFNY JU H XUGOPJKD

GAXDUXWAO XHF HXJPHSSV JDHZKS HWKHL AF JAGK HFL YWHZK

RKHDL WHADY JWHJ LUFJ KZKF KIAYJ VKJ

—LHZK RHDDV

## 12.8

BSF GHBHWF LPZBFWZ DG BFKSEDNDTI MXNN
SPJF BD AF NXTSB—SFPWBFC PEC XEBFNNXTFEB BSF
LPKSXEF FPZXNI LPZBFWZ BSF TWXL PEC BSF CHLA
—LPWZSPNN LKNHSPE

## 12.9

R BFPS RYJZYS SQZY TXRS FYSRG AXY
OIAZP XDIFYM SI YZZMRYE TQXS RJZ RYJZYSZM
—D UFOVARYPSZD WFGGZD

## 12.10

GOZ QFNXBXH NY OVCTXM BM NX CNMG NY GOZ
FBMGM NY GOBXHM GN LNSSE TUNVG YSNC MQBZXQZ
TFNXH LBGO UZOTDBNVS QNXGSNF HZXZGBQ
ZXHBXZZSBXH GSTXMAFTXGZR OZTRM QNCAVGZS ANZGSE
TXR GOZ VXSZMGSTBXZR HSNLGO NY AFTMGBQ YFNLZSM
—FZLBM GONCTM

## 12.11

ADLXUXJD ACHDR FDNFTD XTT ACZEDACZXUR
ACHDR ZEDA RCL ZEDNTNVQ ACHDR ZEDA RXJWST
—ACOZXJ TSZEDO

BXYMOOBF VMIG GMW TMCB WBUWBW KSU BQOEZDBW IGB
YUMCBDWB SDZYUF GMK SUF ASEEW IGB SFCBUIYDB WAMBUAB
—BFVMU OZVBEE GYNNEB

I VIMF KG I GKLCTP GFIFPLPYF FNIF PZPQERYP OPTKPZPG
KF KG KYYRMPYF WYTPGG VRWYX SWKTFE I NECRFNPGKG KG I
YRZPT GWSSPGFKRY FNIF YR RYP HIYFG FR OPTKPZP KF KG
SWKTFE WYFKT VRWYX PVVPMFKZP
—PXHIQX FPTTPQ

KJQHMJH QK OSQBR SC TW WYJRK YK Y LTSKH QK OSQBR
TW KRTMHK OSR YM YJJSPSBYRQTM TW WYJRK QK MT PTUH Y
KJQHMJH RLYM Y LHYC TW KRTMHK QK Y LTSKH
—LHMUQ CTQMJYUH

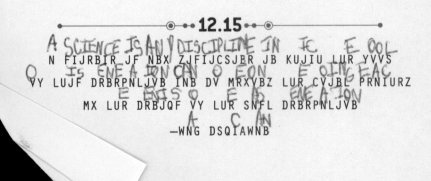

N FIJRBIR JF NBX ZJFIJCSJBR JB KUJIU LUR YVVS
VY LUJF DRBRPNLJVB INB DV MRXYBZ LUR CVJBL PRNIURZ
MX LUR DRBJQF VY LUR SNFL DRBRPNLJVB
—WNG DSQIAWNB

## 12.16

PVS OXDSAPDOP DO AMP H CSZOMA FVM EDBSO PVS ZDEVP
HAOFSZO VSO MAS FVM HOYO PVS ZDEVP IWSOPDMAO
—XNHWJS NSBD—OPZHWOO

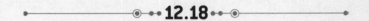

## 12.17

TEICAFC AC GSXEOGSXAFSP MRX ZOFSBCO QO
YMRQ CR GBFE SZRBX XEO TEICAFSP QRLPU ZBX
ZOFSBCO QO YMRQ CR PAXXPO AX AC RMPI AXC
GSXEOGSXAFSP TLRTOLXAOC XESX QO FSM UACFRWOL
—ZOLXLSMU LBCCOPP

## 12.18

HPZ MLSEHLK JN HPSH ZKUSTTSNNJER GJHHGZ YJZIZ
WO HPTZSF HPSH SGVSDN PSERN CTWK HPZ NVZSHZT WO
NYSIZ—HJKZ YLGG JH SEF HPZ VFWGZ HPJER LETSCZGN
—OTZF SGSE VWGO

## 12.19

HU G QGAC MHY XP MGAOPDHAS
IPY WHQ CYTON YWP QGYWPQGYHEC
—UDGAEHC XGEJA

## 12.20

HEE IJHI VEYIIRQN GHX FWI UR VWES UZI

HI ERHNI YI PWFIHYFN TQRR RERPIQWFN

—DWJF SRNGWFS UHRQFHE

## 12.21

GW TEDZPQ KFCW RFYW BDK KD XFCW KEW LBKWPPWRK DZY UDQ

LK EFT DH RDZYTW ADGWYHZP XZTRPWT OZK BD AWYTDBFPLKM

—FPOWYK WLBTKWLB

## 12.22

MGZVZ CQ PRZ MGCRB ZYZR APVZ YCMLN MP QJCZRJZ MGLR

CRMZNNCBZRM AZMGPIQ LRI MGLM CQ MGZ QCRJZVZ IZQCVZ MP

UCRI PXM MGZ MVXMG KGLMZYZV CM ALT HZ

—JGLVNZQ QLRIZVQ SCZVJZ

## 12.23

YLJC CMZM KFQZW ZWMQWJO ZJCOFCT SR MZWQACMSWZ WLJE

BSFIXHE OFZIADJQJO WLMW GMHHRAFCW RJCZ YASHO CAW YAQX

FC UJQA TQMDFWE WA IANGMW WLFZ RQAGHJN CMZM ZIFJCWFZWZ

ZRJCW M OJIMOJ MCO WYJHDJ GFHHFAC CAHHMQZ OJDJHARFCT M

RJC WLMW YQFWJZ FC UJQA TQMDFWE SRZFOJ OAYC SCOJQ

YMWJQ AC MHNAZW MCE ZSQKMIJ FCIHSOFCT THMZZ MCO MW

WJNRJQMWSQJZ QMCTFCT KQAN GJHAY KQJJUFCT WA ADJQ WLQJJ

LSCOQJO IJCWFTQMOJ WLJ QSZZFMCZ SZJO M RJCIFH

—SQGMC HJTJCO

# 12.24

FPD ODDQDGF GXC RERXCGF FPD PTSRC SXCO XG FZ JD♥XDAD
FPXCEG HXFPZTF DAXODCLD GLXDCLD XG GXSQYU LZSSZC GDCGD
RF XFG JDGF FPRF XG KXEXOYU RLLTKRFD XC ZJGDKARFXZC
RCO SDKLXYDGG FZ BRYYRLU XC YZEXL
—FPZSRG PTNYDU

# 12.25

PTJE DWX UAJ QWXAKFEZ U EFQJ ZFAV UE TWXA BJJOB ♥FGJ U
BJQWER PTJE DWX BFK WE U AJR TWK QFERJA U BJQWER BJJOB
VFGJ UE TWXA KTUKB AJVUKFNFKD
—UVHJAK JFEBKJFE

# 12.26

CKB IKJEB KMRCJOD JN RWMBAWB KVR HBBA CKB FOVXYVE
OBVEMGVCMJA CKVC BTBACR XJ AJC KVSSBA MA VA VOHMCOVOD
ZVAABO HYC CKVC CKBD OBNEBWC V WBOCVMA YAXBOEDMAF
JOXBO IKMWK ZVD JO ZVD AJC HB XMTMABED MARSMOBX
—RCBSKBA KVIUMAF

SX XIBCWYCWX TDIV LWBSLWKY YUW RSKTFSTW TDIVX LWBSLWKY

YII VIDLX SDW FXWL YI LCXTFCXW KIY YI CRRFHCKSYW

SBYCIK ZIF RCEWDSYW S BCYZ EZ LWXYDIZCKT CY VIDLX SDW

YI BIKMFXW XI YUSY SY WRWBYCIK YCHW NWINRW VCRR

XIRWHKRZ GIYW STSCKXY YUWCD IVK CKYWDWXYX

—TIDW GCLSR

MU DULUH IJEF YDLUIJYWQJYDW MU QHU DULUH IQJYIVYUT

JXQJ MU ADEM UDEKWX JE WUJ RO ULUHO GKUIJYED MU QDIMUH

BUQTI ED JE QDEJXUH GKUIJYED JXYI XQI RUSECU JXU

WHUQJUIJ IKHLYLQB JHYSA EV EKH IFUSYUI

—TUICEDT CEHHYI

MCAVAPWNPKPMCABVOPICWDCPNMKMANPMCKMPWTPASAVPKJOBJAPGWN

DBSAVNPAQKDM

OPICKMPMCAPRJWSAVNAPWNPTBVPKJGPICOPWMPWNPCAVAPWMPIW

PWJNMKJM OPGWNKEEAKVPKJGPHAPVAE

KDAGPHOPNBLAMCWJYPASAJPLBVAPHWFKVVAPKJGPWJAQE WDKH

APMCAVAPWNPKJBMCAVPMCABVOPICWDCPNMKMANPMCKMPMCWNPCKNPK

VAKGOPCKEEAJAG

—GBRY KNPKGKLN

MEXNUNVXMEZIKFYLLSUAMEZFXSF SANUEFYVXUSES
NUVFVWYLNFMVFTMEMXNFXQMVFMVFYFRNUKFLS
TSUXMEZFXQSJZQXFWYUXMLJIYUIKFTSUFWNSWINFGQSFLYEFENRNUF
UN N DNUFGQNUNFXQNKFQYRN FINTXFXQMEZVFGSSAKFYIJNE

## 12.31

OWMKHMORHYHMJZMZWKHORJPFMZVAHYDENMZNKDWEJBMJPMORHMLTBO
MORTOMTPMTZOYWPTVOMZHPOMVAMTZMTZZJZOTPOMOWMTMZHYJHZMWL
MBWKAVOHYZMLWVPUMORTOMRHMIWYSHUMKWYHMTBBVYTOHENMTPUMKW
YHMJPOHEEJFHPOENMORTPMORHNMTUETJMHMZOHXHPZWP

## 12.32

(Quag) usetheinternet

JTOKU RDCIW MUGOU YBMWL BYAGK WVNSR SDRZJ DNEKU CNTYB
JNWFU QKJKU WSWDK EDCSZ KKPZU HWDKH JBQWY DPBDC NWIXP
FWXGX S

## 12.33

(Quag) emailaddresses

OQEVI MYMBX YZMWZ HNZCN JUXHK TFYEU YUDGX ZNDQG EVRGP
ZJVBJ FAZCV BJHTQ PNVUI KWHJE UUHZP QYMIN WJXJP SPZVN
JJSDB RFJLQ XYIPZ MPFWH YPPJX RIINJ MXFUJ YUYIB VMWHH
NXEMY OPHPD QBJFU PNIEU UHSDR LZSCU DFOFI KZEAS GHNXL
HZPYT GYKVQ HSXDG

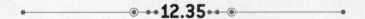

```
AE  SI  NI  IT  UH  OS  OT  IM  HY  OV  NI  GT  OP  NN  SN
MK  NT  ES  EH  LG  TU  RT  EB  CU  ET  OP  NN  SV  NU  LY
IA  DN  WE  EA  IN  RW  UT  AI  FM  LA  WT  IM  XL  NK  NW  CE  TF
CR  TD  EN  TR  UP  BC  NI  CN  IS  PO  ET  AD  AI  GH  ME
TE  IH  BT  AH  RE  AS  IS  PO  ET  EE  TA  LD  EN  AE  GN
RT  OG  OS  PH  TS  AI  IR  IH  TA  PA  CM
```

## 12.35

```
SDTWJL  WAFKLWAF  OZG  VAKUGNWJWV  LZSL  S  LAFQ  SEGMFL

GX  ESKK  AK  WIMSD  LG  S  ZMYW  SEGMFL  GX  WFWJYQ  OZAUZ

WPHDSAFK  OZQ  SK  WAFKLWAF  ZAEKWDX  KG  WDGIMWFLDQ

HML  AL  AF  S  XSEGMK  KHWWUZ  LG  LZW  HZQKAUK  VWHSJLEWFL

SL  HJAFUWLGF  QGM  ZSNW  LG  WPWJUAKW  XGJ  S  OWWC  LG

OGJC  GXX  LZW  LZAYZ  XSL  XJGE  S  KAFYDW  KFAUCWJK

                —VSNW  TSJJQ
```

## 12.36

(Quag) methematica

```
KDIOZ  IPEUP  NZDZD  KESZM  HEUQF  EWWEB  MKHMM  SDKSZ  ZVFFU

FUEAH  EQQWK  HAWOF  OJQTD  JGDUP  PQKSS  UMKEU  IZTAB  NKV
```

## • • 12.37 • •

(Quag) withinstruction

```
OMPKE  KYIWS  TNUWZ  OMVRW  RRIUA  YRJLN  NQWRG  BLWUH  HMVWG
AMWOM  OZUCK  SMBRJ  OJWOA  AVUMA  RNBDE  FRQNS  YYKDS  WDICA
UKCKG  AACOO  ZRUGE  IZIYD  RRBSZ  YRJOA  UNUSN  RLZPA  AVUMA
RNBVJ  SZCKA  SMVWG  AMWOM  UJUJZ  EAKKS  YYNGM  OLISA  ZJVGD
            KVYNP  RNKGR  DARGZ  ADHNA  NM
```

## • • 12.38 • •

```
JH JG SR JLHFAFGH HS LSHF HEMH IEJBF GSWF XSBNEJLG MAF
AFNSAHFX HS EMDF BFMALFX FLTBJGE PN HS RJRHO ISAXG PGFX
JL USAAFUH USLHFZH LS EPWML QFJLT EMG QFFL AFNSAHFX HS
          EMDF BFMALFX XSBNEJLFGF
              —UMAB GMTML
```

## • • OUR TOWN • •

Following is an apropos cryptogram using ancient Babylonian cuneiform characters. The single-letter third word is A.

# SPORTS

"WE DIDN'T LOSE THE GAME;
WE JUST RAN OUT OF TIME."
—*Vince Lombardi*

## 13.1

GU UXXD LY CYOYKUYYK BYMNC UX HYU

UWNYY UWXECMKJ WGUC GK FMCYFMII G JGJ GU

GK XKY MPUYNKXXK XK UWY HXIP TXENCY

—WMKD MMNXK

## 13.2

GESZ DBVTS IKMDNZO MOMNZJF M JFMQPSY YSQP QBCISFS

SUSZ EMTYST JEBG FES GBTKY EBG CVQE DBVKK XNOEF XBT

FES GNZZSTJ QNTQKS NX DBV YB JBCSYMD FES QSKKBIEMZS

GNKK QTMQPKS BXX M XTSJE IMQP BZS FEMF WSKBZOJ FB

DBV MZY FES QMTYJ GNKK WS JFMQPSY NZ DBVT XMUBT

—IMF TNKSD

## 13.3

NGM YDPFPN NGM JPKK NX JPS RSC NGM JPKK NX
MTIMK RFM NGM NGPSBY NGRN MSCZFM NGMYM HZRKPNPMY RFM YX
VZIG VXFM PVDXFNRSN NGRS NGM MUMSNY NGRN XIIZF

—UPSIM KXVQRFCP

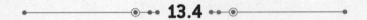

## 13.4

HF PU DFCGWK GZ NGLU T DTNNUH UCEUMH HAUOUZ WF
PRZGE WF EAFOUFKOTMAV TWX HAU XTWEUOZ AGH UTEA FHAUO

—BTEL ATWXV

## 13.5

HGBCUARQV BZJQX CBOJ AQ XGJ LMCV
HGBCUARQV BZJ CBOJ EZRC VRCJXGAQL XGJM GBKJ
OJJU AQVAOJ XGJC B OJVAZJ B OZJBC B KAVARQ

—CIGBCCBO BTA

## 13.6

J APJO QWSZZV JK OSB QJEOS DTINB HBWIPQB ZY GKBPLZKJI
KZO HBWIPQB J SIN JO HPO HBWIPQB J WZPVNKO QGBVV JO

—TZWMR DTIUJIKZ

## 13.7

SRXELU XVZCFYX FZC HOLLT EH TRO SRXC FV
VNC ACUELLELU TRO UCV RHH VR F AFP XVFZV EH TRO
SRXC EL VNC WEPPSC RH VNC XCFXRL TROZC EL F
XSOWD EH TRO SRXC FV VNC CLP TROZC KNRYELU

—UCLC WFOKN

## 13.8

O UFCUVK PIGD PY PST KQYGPK KTMPOYD ZOGKP
PST KQYGPK QUNT GTMYGEK QTYQFTK UMMYRQFCKSRTDPK
PST ZGYDP QUNT SUK DYPSODN LIP RUDK ZUOFIGT⟨
—TUGF CUGGTD

## 13.9

GPX KTYYXWXVZX LXGHXXV GPX QCK LICCBCINXW
IVK GPX VXH LICCBCINXW TD GPX FXWDXN GPX QCK
LICCBCINXW ZIWXK ILQMG GPX VISX QV GPX YWQVG GPX VXH
LICCBCINXW ZIWXD ILQMG GPX VISX QV GPX LIZ⟨
—DGXUX RIWUXN

H SEQL VARHAKA NYEWAXXHEQOR OLDRALAX XDEZRS VA YERA
FESARX H VARHAKA NOYAQLX XDEZRS VA YERA FESARX HLX QEL
RHCA HL TOX TDAQ H TOX BYETHQB ZN FU FEF OQS FU
BYOQSFELDAY LERS FA DET HL TOX BEHQB LE VA HW H SHSQL
RHCA HL LDAU XOHS SEQL RAL LDA SEEY DHL UEZ HQ LDA OXX
EQ UEZY TOU EZL NOYAQLX DOKA LE LOCA VALLAY JEQLYER

—JDOYRAX VOYCRAU

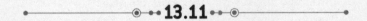

LOBA IBDBJDSR KDNIBVV3V BAEBD QAEN
VKNDEV HNG VESDE VIDBLQAT GK QEV RQPB EOB
INAVEQEGEQNA LOQIO VSHV VBKSDSEB IOGDIO SAM
VESEB HNG OSXB EN VBKSDSEB CQAM SAM JNMH

—JQRR RBB

HTFIF KY ZQ IQQP KZ GQWI PKZC
MQI ZFXOHKUF HTQWXTHY HTF AWYKFI GQW
JFFR GQWIYFNM LKHT HTF ROIHKVWNOIY
QM YTQH OYYFYYPFZH OZC FEFVWHKQZ HTF
NFYY VTOZVF GQWI PKZC TOY HQ CLFNN QZ HTF
FPQHKQZON HTKY KY YTFFI KZHFZYKHG

—SOVJ ZKVJNOWY

## 13.13

YIJ HYJIAH DIU D AJNQC RNHVBUHH ZCUACUI
GJNIU VB RDHURDTT EJJARDTT JI HJWUACVEQ UTHU
RNA ZCUB GJNIU INBBVBQ DIJNBP ACU RDHUH
DEAUI CVAAVBQ D CJWU INB JI KNWYVBQ NY DBP PJZB DEAUI
D AJNSCPJZB D TVAATU RJG SJWUH AJ ACU HNIEDSU

—IJG SDWYDBUTTD

## 13.14

EX ZGS QLUJN L MLDO EUI XSK EX ZGS RHLZ EU
EUI BOJBOLUEGK EX ZGS QGBW LU EU EUI MGHX

—TGT NGRO

## 13.15

TVKYTVSS ZK VSBFKJ JGY FWSO FLNYLSO JGZWC ZW V AYLO
PWFLNYLSO IFLSN ZE OFP CYJ JGLYY KJLZQYK YAYW JGY TYKJ
SVIOYL ZW JGY IFLSN XVWJ CYJ OFP FEE

—TZSS AYYXQ

## 13.16

KC ZPR VOX YVRFIB PW V FPDC YPROAX TROKWF
V ABPOJ VWT VOX VCOVKT PC DKFIBWKWF IPDT RQ
V PWX KOPW WPB XEXW FPT YVW IKB V PWX KOPW

—DXX BOXEKWP

G ZGDIXKL BOHB GZ G AHGL GB KVSIDO G JSIFL

WSVEGVWK BOK JSXFL BOHB G XKHFFR JHA BOK DXKHBKAB

—PIOHPPHL HFG

(Quag) sevenpound

WDPUB OMQQG VNLQH PIHMD NUWQP HHHFJ ESGOF ZIJYS DNILN

TYMPF ZCUNF JHSDB WQNRY YMBFP PFHSP TYFTA HBYIK ARCIN

IIGSW KMIWA FZKBZ ITQWP NDYGR JNEIH KTJIK NKFYS SNHMN

YYJVM HSSNN HVLDB IQYIQ MRQWO RHPCN KFXIM OZQN

(Quag) kitchentable

JAUIN NVHLM JOQNS UTFFI GJJUX FZBAG MJPAZ JJMKN DYJHH

EFQTJ JMSAP JLMFM PENIJ UXZDZ BUCKY OZKKR MPHGY KAEOP

ZHUCX CITQB CDIQV NFGEP AVRJM QNOLS FMKAQ JJUBE TLHLC

JTOLJ ICGXA NVEQE DEGZW AGVKH YJJKP KCTRT BEFQV EGMBY

PJQVH CNOVH ICOUZ HHMWE KPZIJ ETYLB KEUJA EMGTH XFRH

ITN BYS NLD EEL SOK IGR MOG IGO UMK DAE CCO EIL

THM AKO COL IED DOI ERB NOT YIN YPA TWT HLI YBA

## 13.21

```
ARBE  HBSN  AMDT  IWEE  IHET  OTTC  LEIS  EVTT  EEOI
HEFM  NDIA  ISEF  SGOB  LDNC  NTEV  AAIO  NHJS  EEKL
MCNL  EHTY  RRFE  MOAT  ATOS  AFRH  NUDI  EONG  ORCN
HNML  GONI  BAAI  AANR  ROTT  OILK  UMLD  GIHN
```

## 13.22

```
FGHH  HHTI  NRTI  PYFT  EHIN  ICMT  ASIT  EAOS  OEWY
ENOF  NMLT  OROA  HHRT  ORSI  SUOE  NITS  GECA  NHEA
TRTE  EIII  FURF  ESBR  OEHM  RFIR  CWMU  HSCO  EREV
```

## 13.23

(Quag) swingingfor

```
YOWPX  IPRVQ  PGCBM  XWOPG  WKUKH  CWUDT  VWLRH  RRDVK  CPCDV
KDAWU  HUGWQ  VJRIC  SWVPR  VRVVK  DAWDH  WABGM  CRAPC  YWQTG
HPCRH  WQPDC  BNCZG  PFPTI  HHURH  JWDJQ  RVUMM  VPMVP  HWTWV
KDAWT  NHMVR  LWQHB  UDAVW  ERHYR  DFQMC  RVNBW  VKDAW  VUBGK
                            QIVP
```

# • • *ANOTHER CRYPTARITHM* • •

          DICE

+       ODDS

+       BAD
_____

=    LOSES

To arrive at a unique solution,
A = 6, B = 5, and I = 9

# WAR & PEACE

"THERE WAS NEVER A GOOD WAR OR A BAD PEACE." —*Benjamin Franklin*

## 14.1

QC JEGXSVMIW QEC QEOI ER IRH SJ AEV WSSRIV
XLER CSYV GSRKVIWWIW XLI HEC ALIR XAS EVQC GSVTW
GER ERRMLMPEXI IEGL SXLIV MR SRI WIGSRH EPP
GMZMPMDIH REXMSRW MX MW XS FI LSTIH AMPP VIGSMP
JVSQ AEV ERH HMWGLEVKI XLIMV XVSSTW

—EPJVIH RSFIP

## 14.2

WAO ARR SPL SEI DEP SSE EAO ATT LSE AHS TKE HOW YEE
TNT DYT COS ODO EAH EDT DSA RNU TRO EES ESH OHR EDT
TTL XIC INE UHP WHV TEI DMO AEH RGT HIE ODA LNS DAA
SAN TAO PAT HLN TTL SOE NOT OEE WOM TIC COL

CNFTDANSFYX

FWTCFVIMUNYYVPNFMTCNUFVYFGKAFVFRTFSTAFDVSRFVAFVIMUNYYV

PNFXAFXQQFAWNFJKSYFXSRFAWNFGTIGYFAWNFUTHLNAYFXSRFAWNFC

XUYWVMYFXUNFXQQFY IGTQYFTDFWKIXSFDXVQKUNFAWN

FXUNFSNHNYYXU FY IGTQYFAWN

FMUTANHAFCWXAFCNFHWNUVYWFGKAFAWN

FXUNFCVASNYYFATFWKIXSFDTQQ

—Q SRTSFGXVSNYFETWSYTS

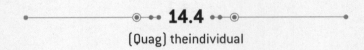

## 14.4
(Quag) theindividual

ZIGHJ HVOPV EVKPY ZBTDD JPOXK KSKBU XDHRV GIORV YXJMK

KSPMS LWKXV YWCMT CYXMQ TDWWN CNAHN YXWSV YXTMB MPKXQ

ZFYQV MQFSJ MEZHB GJHNV XFSJV YJSWV TXJMH KFTAN MWYQQ

ZDZXZ ISWWZ ZBTNQ FXKYD MWSMT HWXHF DXTHT KJGOV CCTWR

UQIYQ QXJHH YHTYU ISWHD CVQFS LXYMF XJCVV ISWHD MQFSJ

MEZHB BITVZ PFXQZ SWGVW ZIGCQ DIGSG CQFAV BDWYO TFR

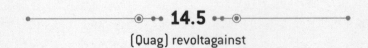

## 14.5
(Quag) revoltagainst

FMNDE HJDNT PDCXB NKNIZ LDEPZ BWJAC TKOQA LNKHW SQNHW

ZBOIL HKGSF MASPF OQYFM YPIMJ YRRPA VSFML PACGW RMDIC

JDRTJ BNSSK FRKJA XPTZR DMDFK KOIMS LVZJS WNEUV OMWBO

UQICW BERRB JSDLK ZRQYN VZGQF JTLKK TMUWC VRQSC NKFPI

KMICP TGTSO KFIIJ GHIRY OC

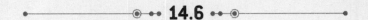

## 14.6

```
HS OY EC EU TA MN NN TO SE AE IE YN EH YA EX AS
EA LT EA TR AI EA BE AI TR TA HS SH TE AD AI WB
HV WS LO CT EH VE HU TD LO HR LE NT VS BA BN
```

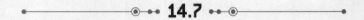

## 14.7

```
YHOFELJXVWJTDWRKVXWJVWD
VVDZXHJFWXEWVXJTXHZSWJWAJTWJVWV
EFYHDTVWJTDWNETWNHZHVGHZSWHXWQEKWXJCDWYHOFELJ
QWEKXWENWAJTWJZYWXGDWXGHZS  WAEKFYWNJFFWNFJXWHZWJWADDC
—AHFFWTESDTV
```

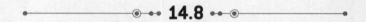

## 14.8

```
S RSM AZE BSJB VZSV ME OSVNQEV BZEXKT SVVSHC VZW
ASN XMVQK QV QB EDWN QB BSJQMP ME PEET BEM BZEXKT ASNM
ZQB REVZWN EY S HKQYY XMVQK BZW ZSB YSKKWM
—PC HZWBVWNVEM
```

## 14.9

```
EKR VOHE EKOE EKR EOIX UON LR LJQFAY JQ
ESQYFZ JQ SAFAGWFQFAY GKJSIZ AJE HOSGR SG EJ VJQYRE
EKR VOHE EKOE FE FG WQRVRQOLIR EJ BOQ
—KRAQN HOLJE IJZYR MQ
```

## 14.10

ICPK HVZCSZKS MGBPTZV QCK MZZP YP

SVUYPH SL ICDZ AZCFZ XYSQ SQZ KDYZK YPKSZCT

LE ICDYPH AZCFZ XYSQ QYK PZYHQMLVK

—ZGMZVS QBMMCVT

## 14.11

T UXTKY UXJU SRBSVR EJKU SRJQR GB LNQX

UXJU BKR BC UXRGR FJZG MBPRAKLRKU XJF IRUURA

MRU BNU BC UXRTA EJZ JKF VRU UXRL XJPR TU

—FETMXU RTGRKXBERA

# • • PIGPEN CIPHER • •

The Pigpen Cipher (sometimes called the Masonic cipher or Freemason's cipher) is not a letter substitution cipher. Instead, it replaces each letter with a symbol. Each letter of the alphabet is placed into grids, usually two different types, each of which is used twice. The grids can be set up anyway a person likes. Here is an example:

| A | B | C |
|---|---|---|
| D | E | F |
| G | H | I |

| J | K | L |
|---|---|---|
| M | N | O |
| P | Q | R |

S / T O / V (X-grid)

W / X Y / Z (X-grid with dots)

Using the above example, here is a quote from a well-known American humorist.

A= ⌐  B= ⊔  J= ⌐·  N= ▣  Y= ◁  Z= ◬

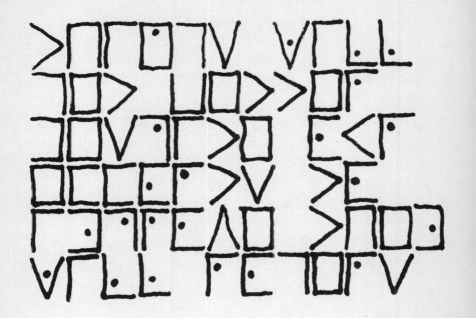

# WORDS
## OF WISDOM

IT IS EASIER TO BE WISE FOR
OTHERS THAN FOR OURSELVES.
—*Francois de La Rochefoucauld*

### 15.1

WOD KGUMQDR XVWO KDUKQD XOU OELD IU LVNDF
VF WOEW ZDIDGEQQC CUP NEI MD KGDWWC FPGD WODCGD
ZUVIZ WU OELD FURD KGDWWC EIIUCVIZ LVGWPDF
—DQVTEMDWO WECQUG

### 15.2

CGWD LJ QND IKTZ OAGTLQZ PNLBN NGJ VDMQ UD IC GKZHIEZ
L NGFD DFDC JQAELDE PCLQLKW BITAUKJ SIC KDPJMGMDCJ
—YLUUZ HCDJTLK

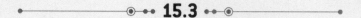

## 15.3

FSS AHK FMT SBPG DTSDPT CMS XBSC MSC FS OZB FMT

RSZBFOG HOT AZWG KOEYEBI RHAW HBK RZFFEBI MHEO

—ITSOIT AZOBW

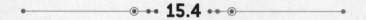

## 15.4

P QKKG CDBVU CPYXGCIKR UEK SCH P QKKG

CDBVU APKUR PU RKKTR UB TK UEKH CYK SBIAKYQVG

UEPINR QBY BUEKY XKBXGK UB NB BI

—OKCI JKYY

## 15.5

E RHB CW HLLDCLEWC NGHLDTDO LW HCBYWQBJ

ROHEJD WO YZHSD E JESRZB KWZZWN SB WNC KDDZECFJ

—NWZKFHCF HSHQDVJ SWMHOL

## 15.6

P JPQ XQNC NHPAQW TQ OVX VPCW XQH MC AHPFTQY

PQF OEH XOEHA MC PWWXGTPOTXQ VTOE WJPAOHA BHXBNH

—VTNN AXYHAW

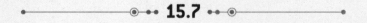

## 15.7

L VBZF QMLTBDBZF PBC BZNJGOMSMZNM NLZ MBSPMQ

UMTMFLSM JQ LYUBNLSM PBC UESBMC L WLSPMQ NLZ UJ ZMBSPMQ

—GLQTMZM UBMSQBNP

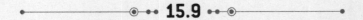

## 15.8

ODERQLS QE D OLGI LO ZUAQSVEE EL QSCLAVGDWAV
CRDC KV RDBV CL DACVG QC VBVGJ EQH ILSCRE
—LEYDG KQAFV

## 15.9

EPYO KDJ BYSQDAY NX BXZY ZIBNYSDXRB
TYDNI JYSZDNB CYBNDUKDNI XO EYTOYBTUI UOT
UCBXKRNDXO XO BROTUI AUBP ZY XRN
—HSUOG BDOUNSU

## 15.10

ZGS PBO LBTQWZ BLLSKQ NIBN ZGSFQ PDQBNQE
HGE UO ZGSD GYO UKBHQ YIQO UN NSDOL GSN NIBN
HGE IBNQL BWW NIQ LBKQ JQGJWQ ZGS EG
—BOOQ WBKGNN

## 15.11

PHGTE UJP KYEPZ UJPORZEB UJP CJHG
KYEPZ UJPO GTNZ PHGTE UJP KYEPZ UJPO GTNZ
UJP CTEE HJG QJ YHUGVTHF CTGV TG
—N RMJGG DZMA

## 15.12

KEGD EX INEIKN JQWG GE BPTN JPGS LEH PW

GSN KPOE CHG JSQG LEH JQWG PD DEONEWN JSE JPKK GQRN

GSN CHD JPGS LEH JSNW GSN KPOE CBNQRD TEJW

—EIBQS JPWXBNL

## 15.13

V ZBMZUI IG MWRR IYCGNOY IYVR FGCHQ ANI GPUZ

WPT OGGQ IYZCZKGCZ IYWI V UWP QG GC WPT EVPQPZRR

GC WAVHVIVZR IYWI V UWP RYGF IG WPT KZHHGF

UCZWINCZ HZI LZ QG VI PGF HZI LZ PGI QZKZC VI GC

PZOHZUI VI KGC V RYWHH PGI MWRR IYVR FWT WOWVP

—FVHHVWL MZPP

## 15.14

ILVVDII QI HEJ JAD GDK JE AYXXQHDII

AYXXQHDII QI JAD GDK JE ILVVDII QC KEL MEWD

FAYJ KEL YTD SEQHU KEL FQMM RD ILVVDIICLM

—YMRDTJ IVAFDQJBDT

## 15.15

UX NSXIQ HAA VWB MOTX NXHBRYOIC EVB

NXRWBOMD HIQ MYXI UX YHMX OM UYXI UX CXM OM

—FVYI NMXOIKXRL

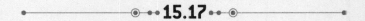

## 15.16

VJW RB J BYNLRJU KNRWP JWM RO UNOC
CX QRVBNUO RW JW RBXUJCNM LXWMRCRXW FXDUM
KN XWN XO CQN FNJTNBC LANJCDANB KDC
JBBXLRJCNM FRCQ QRB TRWM QN FXATB FXWMNAB
—MJWRNU FNKBCNA

## 15.17

OZXYNHJ NX F HTRRTINYD BMNHM NS F RTWJ
TW QJXX FIZQYJWFYJI HTSINYNTS YMJ XYFYJ XJQQX
YT YMJ HNYNEJS FX F WJBFWI KTW MNX FQQJLNFSHJ
YFCJX FSI UJWXTSFQ XJWANHJ
—FRGWTXJ GNJWHJ

## 15.18

KZJKGZ CVQZ OJ OVGF VWJPO NJHZOCDIB EPNO
OJ FZZK OCZDM QJDXZ WJSZN DI RJMFDIB JMYZM NJ
OCZTGG CVQZ BJJY QJDXZ WJSZN DI XVNZ OCZMZV
ZQZM VITOCDIB MZVGGT HZVIDIBAPG OJ NVT
—FPMO QJIIZBPO EM

## 15.19

ODQJXDJH LV WKH DUPRUB RI WKH KXPDQ PLQG
DQG DW RQFH FRQWDLQV WKH WURSKLHV RI LWV SDVW
DQG WKH ZHDSRQV RI LWV IXWXUH FRQTXHVWV
—VDPXHO WDBORU FROHULGJH

## 15.20

```
GTECGE TU JXAM TUZ KBKT GRIUNUR IGAYKY
ZNK LATJGSKTZGR ORRY UL YUIOKZE OL CKXK RUUQOTM
LUX ZNK YUAXIK UL UAX ZXUAHRKY CK YNUARJTZ
ZKYZ VKUVRK LUX JXAMY CK YNUARJ ZKYZ ZNKS LUX
YZAVOJOZE OMTUXGTIK MXKKJ GTJ RUBK UL VUCKX
            —V P UXUAXQK
```

## 15.21

```
PQ OCP ECP RWV C EJCKP CDQWV VJG CPMNG
QH JKU HGNNQY OCP YKVJQWV CV NCUV HKPFKPI VJG
QVJGT GPF HCUVGPGF CDQWV JKU QYP PGEM
         —HTGFGTKEM FQWINCUU
```

## 15.22

```
QEB JBQXMELO LC QEB JBIQFKD MLQ FP
RKCLOQRKXQB XKA JFPIBXAFKD X JLOB XZZROXQB
XKXILDV TLRIA YB X PXIXA YLTI CLO QELRDE
QEB PXIXA FP XK BKQFQV QEB IBQQRZB ZXK PQFII
YB AFPQFKDRFPEBA COLJ QEB ZEFZLOV
      QEB QLJXQLBP COLJ QEB ZXYYXDB
            —ZXOI K ABDIBO
```

## 15.23

KQADVFXSMVZOFCKYFDLSFDUAYOGFQVMTQSFMVFKDJMVZFGKSFJXMUM
GPFGYFUSDLVFRLYAFGKSFSIWSLMSVBSFYRFYGKSLOFDLSFDUOYFLSA
DLEDXUSFRYLFGKSMLFDWWDLSVGFHMOMVBUMVDGMYVFGYFHYFOYF

—HY QZUDOFDHDAO

## 15.24

NPGWNGRNWXLWMWLZDRNWDMNGWZUNGJJZKGUVGWZRWNPGWMHZJZN
WNXWPXJSWNBXWXEEXRGSWZSGMRWMNWNPGWRMOGWNZOGWMUSWRNZJJW
DGNMZUWNPGWMHZJZN WNXWLIUVNZXUW

—LWRVXNNWLZNTKGDMJS

## 15.25

UREOTRGRH GEDREJX UEJUF EXGEFKJFWGEFHEFQQRO FAKREZXS
EJUVEATXHZGEDREHRJGEVSEFEZTRF E UVMZU
EARSVTREMHYHVJHEURERHTXQURGEDREJX UVM
EXDOVPRTXGUXHZEUXDGRKSETFKOUEJFKCVERDRTGVH

## 15.26

AJPEVEGTPNVJUVYDETYTPFVUYJRVEGDVKJYCAVHPETCVEGDVKJYCAV
KTCCVSDVZJYYLVEGWEVLJHVYDETYDVTVGWEDVWVUDCCJKVKGJRVQYT
ADVJYVXJKWYATXDVJYVCWMTPDZZVAYT
DVTPEJVWVXJYPDYVWPAVKGJVAJDZVPJEGTPFVKGDPVGDVTZVEGDYDV
SHEVZTEVWPAVFYJKCVCDEVGTRVXJRDVJHEVNZVTVAJVWPAVSWYN

—Z WRHDCVIJGPZJP

## 15.27

LJVDJXTVLDPVA ZPVGUPQAV LVNJWLMV AVQPVDPXTV
LVLQPFLMVUAVLJVD GPVHPPFVALCRPNUPTVNJWV VABJWPVJNVMP
WAV FTVL YPVW FYVFJLV AV VRWJRDPLVHCLV AV FVCFLP BD
HXPVHW LVQPXXVHUWBDPTV

FTVFJFPVLDPVQUAPW

—WJHPWLVXJCUAVALPGPFAJF

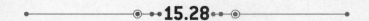

## 15.28

VWJEXBWERGETKWPBBUWELNUQWHJNKBWGJNWPBRVBXBCWHJEHWHJBWQ
ABEHBKHWOABBCNLWNOWK
BBSJWGEKWHJBWQABEHBKHWKEOBHTWPBSEFKBWVOWEWLEUWVKWEWONN
RWHJBWPBKHWHJVUQWHNWCNWVKWHNWBUSNFAEQBWJVLWHNWECXBAHVK
BWHJBWOESHWPTWK BEDVUQWGNNCANGWGVRKNU

## 15.29

AINHVRNHAJNHPJZINHJEMJVOHJPWNHJI
JFHPRLAJRPJVOHJAWNHJKWMJVOWVJZHQVWRPJRPAHZVAJZINHJEMJV
OHJPWNHJI JZHPVRGHBHJPIVJEHZWLAHJVOHMJOWYHJWJOLPBQHBJ
HHVJELVJEHZWLAHJNIAVJGHIGCHJZWPVJZILPVJWEIYHJ

ILQVHHPJ

—FJZJCRZOVHPEHQF

## 15.30

KSDBJLODBYOLIIBKSDBTOGW BKSDBJLODBYMEFMRBVEMMBEKBYLB
LVPBGP BKSDBJLODBYODD EMRBFDBIVGMMLVD
BIEPADBTLMMRBVEMMBGMVGRIBTEP
BTGEKSBVSDODBEJHLIKLOIBVEMMBTEP BEJHOW
DPAD

—ASGOMDIBAGMDFBALMKLP

## 15.31

(Quag) tworeasons

POOZE YRPGM UENFM JKMEN NOAEG QZOPB BMCVS EQAGZ ENOPO
ZCPON EZNIV ENYHY ZMZPI

## 15.32

(Quag) mollyivins

HIEJO OZJBG OTXAK OGAKB WBYCA FBWQM VDHQX ZHEVI ZZIEG
ONGIJ PGZGM WHEDB NBYNA GXMGW QMVJO PAIBB XFJAW GIGKU
ACFFJ RAIIG IGJVQ DYDPL ZV

## 15.33

(Quag) theuniverse

VUKXC DDXFC JCPGH BFCCA FPMOA FLLQI ENKPF SPEKQ TNENK
BQZSC CKCHD QWLMH OUELD YENWL FCAPH XCOJP OQBAE GLAUH
MBOJD ABHSH KJCNN CQAKB LLMH

## 15.34
(Play) theypretend

TVPTVSMGZBARIBPOVBBMBSLUISERIBRYISMGLKTIPJLCJOJVUH
LIVLTSBRKXOZPJITISVESIPJVZKABZLBJKJVVHBSLKTIXGLZSV
ISJBOZZBHRELLU

## 15.35
(Play) happinessis

FZCALFFELBGUGUFDTBEURBVBAFBXZTACTZWAPJELKNAEMSDGRV
OAJVTZBKXOCKFNSIWKTGABPYTHYBDOBLFREWJRPYTHCHMDSZVB
PMFBMHKMAJMGSINZFWOGBARBTCOEAYHMORJDIKFBRJJRTHKCCR
CPEWLHOXPYKBWUWU

## 15.36
(Play) aboutdancing

DBEJDCPUFVKPVIGBHWBCEXFVRYNFJCKCOFNTPLFHOFNSOLFUBT
UEIJSHHPACETZGFCPAHPACRAUODNLGCILSGBHPMGIBDCUOVCXL
PLUVBWBS

## 15.37
(Play) bustlebustle

HLPSLSACUOYFBDGYFTTSLSKINTPHWMUAKMORSRCLLGUTDNTRKF
DNTRKFDNTRKFSLJDNRJTNRJTNRFYGPMKUBSLGKUTCKNRPIUKOS
LHACEKTRSLMBXNSPUKUBBLWFKGBLJAUOCYLABLCUXAUZTRAICA
BLJSNCJPSCGKHOKFZY

## 15.38

(Play) betterbook

AJSLSOASOXDCCHTOHCCHODNWRLKBFCTETOHCCHNCKELNBNNKCL
FCRHSYCHNKDLCGCBTLBPSOJTNGJCHJDNBCFBMJGYJFDPAUBJCT
FBMIJCBSJFAFNRTIJFAFOKOZAUMPCLFCRHSIGRLTBPABJTINNW
NOOCMUFYOWRNGKKEANGS

## 15.39

(Play) drasticchange

FBDZJRYVKNMGTLJBYJGDERKPJPOKGORGGBRMPXOVFBOYBPSZOK
GHZLWGAOOYOGGMYGNZLXGTONHJYNOKRAOMOUMOAHWFSWORKZPO
HWRHDGVPGPKZKELDPOLYERMRWJTLOMBPYJLHHGMW

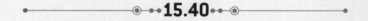

## 15.40

H6 LA RG TH NE AD HT EE RF OH SO YH TA CN EE LA NN
TI GR MI TR GO GB RA DH WE EW SI HW EH SI TA WL AN
RM IT RT AM NA NV RE RA YH NF OH SO YE RE EN RS AR

## 15.41

EE YA TS OT CN EN NF ID IH IT SH VR PS IW RH OD MI
GR ER CN EZ CE

## 15.42

LZW XAJKL XSDD GX KFGO AK FGL GFDQ SF WNWFL AL AK S

ESYAUSD WNWFL QGM YG LG TWV AF GFW CAFV GX S OGJDV SFV

OSCW MH AF SFGLZWJ IMALW VAXXWJWFL SFV AX LZAK AK FGL

WFUZSFLEWFL LZWF OZWJW AK AL LG TW XGMFV

—B T HJAWKLDWQ

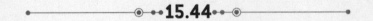

## 15.43

ZNQQ D KDF ZGNJN DJN ZGJNN GCFBJNB OWQQWEF YZDJY WF

ZGN CFWINJYN DFB GNQQ ONQWNIN UEC ZNQQ GWK D ONFTG GDY

MNZ LDWFZ EF WZ DFB GNQQ GDIN ZE ZECTG WZ ZE ON YCJN

—DQONJZ NWFYZNWF

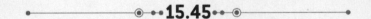

## 15.44

SA LMK DKTHC JCMJXC LMK NOUC RM QSGC QM XMUC QNCG

—GMQNCY QCYCFO

## 15.45

QDKDN PDRR VDUVRD MUG PU IU PMTQHC PDRR PMDL GMEP PU

IU EQI PMDA GTRR CSNVNTCD AUS GTPM PMDTN TQHDQSTPA

—HDUNHD CLTPM VEPPUQ

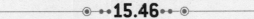

## 15.46

AS KO PWSTIOF ZE TSACZTI
QTXOEE BSQ YSTAZTQO AS
WONONKOW ZA -YSTMQYZQE

## 15.47

UFDJTRF YF KWPI IZGPQ JUWTI XTITAF
OFPFAJIGWPR IZFC YGVV PFMFA XWAOFI TR
—ZFPAGQ IGQQJPFP

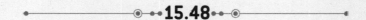

## 15.48

MJT OWMKAKEM KE CUM MJT FOC GJU EOQE MJT LKATL KE
SKLMQ MJT OWMKAKEM KE MJT FOC GJU WNTOCE IB MJT LKATL
—LUEE BTLUM

## 15.49

UWJWBU ID RCSGBH OZKOMG ASOB MCI OFS KSOY GCASHWASG
WH ASOBG HVOH MCI OFS GHFCBU SBCIUV HC ZSH LC
—OBCB

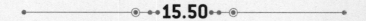

## 15.50

MJ CSY VINIGX XLI JSSH MKRSVI XLI
GYWXSQW JIEV XLI VIPMKMSR ERH EZSMH XLI
TISTPI CSY QMKLX FIXXIV WKEC LSQI
—NEQIW QMGLIRIV

# ••STICKLINKS••

Below is a StickLink cryptogram. Starting with the letter in the circle, link the letters together horizontally, vertically, and/or diagonally to come up with the hidden message.

```
W    E    U    Z    L    S    E    A    D    U    T    R    Y

H    O    P    H    Z    E    W    H    A    O    E    R    S

P    Y    E    T    D    L    A    B    Y    R    O    I    T

E    O    N    J    E    L    K    I    T    H    F    K    C

U    E    O    Y    M    A    N    G    E    M    S    L    E
```

(W)_ ____ ___ _____ ___ _____ ,

__ ___ _ ____ _____ ____ ___ ___ ,

-_____ _____

# HINTS

THIS section contains hints for the Quiptics, Playfair, and Quagmire puzzles. For the Quiptics puzzles, we have given you the letter equivalent of the "space." For the Playfair cryptograms, we've provided the keyword. For the Quagmire ciphers, we've provided a keyword key, cipher key, indicator key and indicator column number. The indicator is shown as EXAMPLE /12 where EXAMPLE is the indicator key, and the number following the slash, in this case 12, is the column location of the indicator key. Columns are numbered from left to right.

**1.3** • *Key:* KENNELRATION
*Cipher Key:* KENNELRATION
*Indicator:* RAWHIDE /17

**1.4** • *Key:* COMPARISONS
*Cipher Key:* COMPARISONS
*Indicator:* DIGITAL /16

**1.8** • *Key:* COLDNOSES

**1.9** • *Key:* WHATSGOINON

**1.10** • *Key:* CLARINET

**1.11** • *Key:* BORDERLINE

**2.16** • R = SPACE

**2.17** • U = SPACE

**2.18** • *Key:* KILIMANJARO
*Cipher Key:*
*Indicator:* SNOWCAP /17

**2.19** • *Key:*
*Cipher Key:* DICTIONARY
*Indicator:* DEVILS /1

**2.20** • *Key:* GINGERROGERS
*Cipher Key:* GINGERROGERS
*Indicator:* FLIGHT /17

**2.21** • *Key:* NORTHCOAST
*Cipher Key:* NORTHCOAST
*Indicator:* PEOPLE /21

**2.22** • *Key:* COMFORTABLE
*Cipher Key:* COMFORTABLE
*Indicator:* TORPEDO /9

**2.23** • *Key:* KAIJUEIGA

**2.24** • *Key:* CORNFIELD

**3.17** • H = SPACE

**3.18** • L = SPACE

**3.19** • S = SPACE

**3.20** • I = SPACE

**3.21** • *Key:* FORTISSIMO
*Cipher Key:*
*Indicator:* SCHOOL /5

**3.22** • *Key:* CONVERSATIONALIST
*Cipher Key:*
CONVERSATIONALIST
*Indicator:* SIMPLE /12

**3.24** • *Key:* PRESIDENT

**3.32** • *Key:* MACHINERY
*Cipher Key:*
*Indicator:* BULLETS /24

**4.12** • Y = SPACE

**4.13** • I = SPACE

**4.14** • *Key:* PHILADELPHIA
*Cipher Key:*
*Indicator:* LIBERTY /23

**4.15** • *Key:*
*Cipher Key:* TERRYSTICKELS
*Indicator:* PUZZLE /11

**4.16** • *Key:* HOWIRONIC
*Cipher Key:* HOWIRONIC
*Indicator:* WRECKED /22

**4.17** • *Key:* PROJECTION
*Cipher Key:* TELEVISION
*Indicator:* REPAIR /1

**4.18** • *Key:* THEBEATGOESON
*Cipher Key:* SONNYANDCHER
*Indicator:* TVSHOWS /5

**4.19** • *Key:* CHRISTMAS
*Cipher Key:* STOCKING
*Indicator:* SANTAS /13

**4.20** • *Key:* CLOCKWORK
*Cipher Key:* ORANGE
*Indicator:* DELPHI /9

**4.21** • *Key:* CONGRATULATIONS

**4.22** • *Key:* MEMORIES

**4.23** • *Key:* MICKEYMOUSE

**4.24** • *Key:* MARIONETTE

**4.30** • *Key:* CANDYMAN
*Cipher Key:* CANDYMAN
*Indicator:* LOBSTER /1

**4.31** • *Key:* UNIVERSITY
*Cipher Key:*
*Indicator:* GALLONS  /9

**5.10** • *Key:* MEALTIME

**5.11** • *Key:* NANTUCKET
*Cipher Key:*
*Indicator:* WHALER  /1

**5.12** • *Key:* FARMLAND

**5.17** • *Key:* BURGUNDY
*Cipher Key:*
*Indicator:* DECANT  /22

**5.18** • *Key:* BACTERIA
*Cipher Key:*
*Indicator:* DISEASE  /3

**6.24** • V = SPACE

**6.25** • K = SPACE

**6.26** • W = SPACE

**6.27** • S = SPACE

**6.28** • *Key:* CHRISTMAS
*Cipher Key:*
*Indicator:* SCROOGE  /10

**6.29** • *Key:*
*Cipher Key:* CIPHERTEXT
*Indicator:* AUGUST  /3

**6.30** • *Key:* POTBELLIED

**6.38** • H = SPACE

**6.39** • K = SPACE

**6.40** • *Key:* MONTICELLO
*Cipher Key:*
*Indicator:* FOUNDER  /6

**7.14** • Q = SPACE

**7.15** • X = SPACE

**7.16** • Y = SPACE

**7.17** • D = SPACE

**7.18** • E = SPACE

**7.19** • *Key:* DANCELAND
*Cipher Key:* DANCELAND
*Indicator:* FOXTROT  /12

**7.20** • *Key:* PREVARICATE
*Cipher Key:* PREVARICATE
*Indicator:* KEYNOTE  /13

**7.21** • *Key:* POGOPOSSUM

**7.22** • *Key:* WEIGHTY

**7.23** • *Key:* VIOLINIST

**8.22** • *Key:*
*Cipher Key:*
*Indicator:* RODREEL /22

**8.23** • *Key:* DECADENCE

**8.24** • *Key:* SAXOPHONE

**8.25** • *Key:* GENIUS

**8.26** • *Key:* OVERCOME

**8.27** • *Key:* MINUTEMEN

**8.28** • *Key:* ANYMORE

**8.29** • *Key:* RIFLE

**8.31** • *Key:* POETRY
*Cipher Key:* USMINT
*Indicator:* NICKEL /12

**8.32** • *Key:* PEACEPIPE
*Cipher Key:* TELESCOPE
*Indicator:* AWKWARD /18

**8.33** • *Key:* JUPITER
*Cipher Key:*
*Indicator:* BALLOON /6

**9.10** • X = SPACE

**9.11** • *Key:*
*Cipher Key:* PARADISELOST
*Indicator:* MILTON /4

**9.12** • *Key:*
*Cipher Key:* FEMINIST
*Indicator:* MARRIED /20

**9.13** • *Key:* FASCINATING
*Cipher Key:* FASCINATING
*Indicator:* LISTEN /24

**10.20** • U = SPACE

**10.21** • *Key:* SATISFACTION
*Cipher Key:* OKLAHOMA
*Indicator:* PIANO /17

**10.22** • *Key:* MECHANICAL
*Cipher Key:* DRAWING
*Indicator:* PENCIL /16

**11.24** • K = SPACE

**11.25** • W = SPACE

**11.27** • A = SPACE

**11.28** • U = SPACE

**11.29** • *Key:* WASHINGTON
*Cipher Key:* WASHINGTON
*Indicator:* HIGHWAY /2

**11.31** • *Key:* MONOSODIUM
*Cipher Key:* GLUTAMATE
*Indicator:* COOKING /7

**11.32** • *Key:* POSSIBLE
*Cipher Key:* UNICORN
*Indicator:* HORNED /14

**11.33** • *Key:* COMEDIAN

**12.29** • P = SPACE

**12.30** • F = SPACE

**12.31** • M = SPACE

**12.32** • *Key:* COMPUTER
*Cipher Key:* MEGABYTES
*Indicator:* MOUSING /26

**12.33** • *Key:* CONGRESSMAN
*Cipher Key:* SENATOR
*Indicator:* CAPITOL /23

**12.36** • *Key:* TOUPEE
*Cipher Key:* INVENTOR
*Indicator:* WEATHER /20

**12.37** • *Key:* MACHINERY
*Cipher Key:* GEARSHIFT
*Indicator:* METAL /19

**13.18** • *Key:* PUNCHDRUNK
*Cipher Key:*
*Indicator:* ROUNDS /16

**13.19** • *Key:*
*Cipher Key:* SENTIMENTAL
*Indicator:* ALLTIME /7

**13.23** • *Key:* BASEBALL
*Cipher Key:*
*Indicator:* INNING /21

**14.3** • F = SPACE

**14.4** • *Key:*
*Cipher Key:* LABRADCR
*Indicator:* BLACK /23

**14.5** • *Key:* DEMOCRATIC
*Cipher Key:* CHRONICLE
*Indicator:* BITMAPS /7

**14.7** • W = SPACE

**15.23** • F = SPACE

**15.24** • W = SPACE

**15.25** • E = SPACE

**15.26** • V = SPACE

**15.27** • W = SPACE

**15.28** • W = SPACE

**15.29** • J = SPACE

**15.30** • B = SPACE

**15.31** • *Key:* OILWELL
*Cipher Key:* OILWELL
*Indicator:* TUESDAY /10

**15.32** • *Key:* COLUMNIST
*Cipher Key:*
*Indicator:* POLITIC /15

**15.33** • *Key:* LUNATIC
       *Cipher Key:*
       *Indicator:* FRINGE /7

**15.34** • *Key:* SILVERSCREEN

**15.35** • *Key:* LAWNMOWER

**15.36** • *Key:* BELLOTTO

**15.37** • *Key:* PASTRAMI

**15.38** • *Key:* CASTIRON

**15.39** • *Key:* GERMANY

# SOLUTIONS

## •• *CHAPTER ONE: ANIMALS* ••

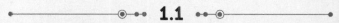
### **1.1**

Man is an animal which, alone among the animals, refuses to be satisfied by the fulfillment of animal desires. —*Alexander Graham Bell*

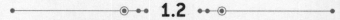
### **1.2**

Every morning in Africa, a gazelle wakes up. It knows it must outrun the fastest lion or it will be killed. Every morning in Africa, a lion wakes up. It knows it must run faster than the slowest gazelle, or it will starve. It doesn't matter whether you are a lion or a gazelle, when the sun comes up, you'd better be running. —*Anon*

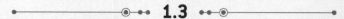
### **1.3**

I got an early impression of retrievers when a friend would mark an orange with his fingernail and throw it on top of a truck full of oranges. Then he'd call his Labrador who would climb onto the truck pick up the marked orange and bring it back. —*Waterman, Gun Dogs and Bird Guns*

### **1.4**

The codfish lays ten thousand eggs. The homely hen lays one. The codfish never cackles to tell you what she's done, and so we scorn the codfish, while the humble hen we prize. Which only goes to show you that it pays to advertise. —*Anonymous*

## 1.5

If you think dogs can't count, try putting three dog biscuits in your pocket and give Fido only two. —*Phil Pastoret*

## 1.6

The dog has seldom been successful in pulling man up to its level of sagacity, but man has frequently dragged the dog down to his. —*James Thurber*

## 1.7

If you want to cure your dog's bad breath, just pour a little Lavoris in the toilet —*Jay Leno*

## 1.8

Nobody can fully understand the meaning of love unless he's owned a dog. He can show you more honest affection with a flick of his tail than a man can gather through a lifetime of handshakes. —*Gene Hill*

## 1.9

Newfoundland dogs are good to save children from drowning, but you must have a pond of water handy and a child, or else there will be no profit in boarding a Newfoundland. —*Josh Billings*

## 1.10

Labradors are lousy watchdogs. They usually bark when there is a stranger about, but it is an expression of unmitigated joy at the chance to meet somebody new, not a warning. —*Norman Strung*

## 1.11

The problem with cats is that they get the exact same look on their face whether they see a moth or an axe-murderer. —*Paula Poundstone*

## 1.12

To a teacher of languages there comes a time when the world is but a place of many words and man appears a mere talking animal not much more wonderful than a parrot. —*Joseph Conrad*

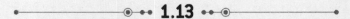

## 1.13

One reason why birds and horses are happy is because they are not trying to impress other birds and horses. —*Dale Carnegie*

## 1.14

Always remember, a cat looks down on man, a dog looks up to man, but a pig will look man right in the eye and see his equal. —*Winston Churchill*

## 1.15

The elephant has a thick skin, a head full of ivory, and as everyone who has seen a circus parade knows, proceeds best by grasping the tail of its predecessor. —*Adlai E. Stevenson*

## 1.16

Scientists tell us that the fastest animal on earth, with a top speed of one hundred twenty feet per second, is a cow that has been dropped out of a helicopter. —*Dave Barry*

## 1.17

Those who admire the massive, rigid bone structures of dinosaurs should remember that jellyfish still enjoy their very secure ecological niche.
—*Beau Sheil*

## 1.18

The reason I love my dog so much is because when I come home, he's the only one in the world who treats me like I'm the Beatles. —*Bill Maher*

# •• *CHAPTER TWO: ART & LITERATURE* ••

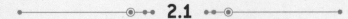

## 2.1

Simplicity is the final achievement. After one has played a vast quantity of notes and more notes, it is simplicity that emerges as the crowning reward of art. —*Chopin*

## 2.2

There are many ways of breaking a heart. Stories were full of hearts broken by love, but what really broke a heart was taking away its dream—whatever that dream might be. —*Pearl Buck*

## 2.3

Most rock journalism is people who can't write, interviewing people who can't talk, for people who can't read. —*Frank Zappa*

## 2.4

A serious writer is not to be confounded with a solemn writer. A serious writer may be a hawk or a buzzard or even a popinjay but a solemn writer is always a bloody owl. —*Ernest Hemingway*

## 2.5

If my husband would ever meet a woman on the street who looked like the women in his paintings he would fall over in a dead faint.
—*Mrs. Pablo Picasso*

## 2.6

Everyone has talent. What is rare is the courage to follow that talent to the dark place where it leads. —*Erica Jong*

## 2.7

If you're a singer you lose your voice. A baseball player loses his arm. A writer gets more knowledge, and if he's good, the older he gets, the better he writes. —*Mickey Spillane*

## 2.8

What I dream of is an art of balance, of purity and serenity devoid of troubling or depressing subject matter, a soothing, calming influence on the mind, rather like a good armchair which provides relaxation from physical fatigue. —*Henri Matisse*

## 2.9

I read and walked for miles at night along the beach, writing bad blank verse and searching endlessly for someone wonderful who would step out of the darkness and change my life. It never crossed my mind that that person could be me. —*Anna Quindlen*

## 2.10

With a jumble of his health, the heat, and the corpses of bees revolving lazily round his mind, James Bond strolled off in the direction of the tall grey building whose upper storeys showed themselves above the trees. It was three-thirty. Only two more hours to go before his next drink.
—*Ian Fleming*

## 2.11

Sunshine is delicious. Rain is refreshing. Wind braces up. Snow is exhilarating. There is no such thing as bad weather, only different kinds of good weather.
—*John Ruskin*

## 2.12

The liberty of the press is a blessing when we are inclined to write against others and a calamity when we find ourselves overborne by the multitude of our assailants. —*Samuel Johnson*

## 2.13

The older we grow the greater becomes our wonder at how much ignorance one can contain without bursting one's clothes. —*Mark Twain*

## 2.14

It's a shame that the only thing a man can do for eight hours a day is work. He can't eat for eight hours. He can't drink for eight hours. He can't make love for eight hours. The only thing a man can do for eight hours is work.
—*William Faulkner*

## 2.15

Once when he was sketching near the sea, a little girl who had fallen into the water walked by with dripping clothes. Lewis Carroll tore a corner from a piece of blotting paper and said, "May I offer you this to blot you up?"
—*Martin Gardner*

## 2.16

Now most successful lawyers took degrees in law, and most successful chemical engineers took degrees in chemical engineering, which at least suggests that their schooling had a direct bearing on their success in their chosen field. Then how come most successful authors took degrees not in English literature but in some widely different field? —*John W. Campbell*

## 2.17

I like nonsense. It wakes up the brain cells. Fantasy is a necessary ingredient in living. It's looking at life through the wrong end of a telescope, which is what I do, and that enables you to laugh at life's realities. —*Dr. Seuss*

## 2.18

Hemingway had a perfected gallows humor. He liked rough jokes with a sting at the end. He once gave me some rules for life, among them: always do sober what you said you'd do when you were drunk. That will teach you to keep your mouth shut. —*Scribner*

## 2.19

Lexicographer. A pestilent fellow who, under the pretense of recording some particular stage in the development of a language, does what he can to arrest its growth, stiffen its flexibility, and mechanize its methods.
—*Ambrose Bierce*

## 2.20

A fumblerule is a mistake that calls attention to the rule. It behooves us to avoid archaisms. Proofread to see if you any words out. Boycott eponyms. Ixnay on colloquial stuff. Zap onomatopoeia. Take the bull by the hand and don't mix metaphors. Never use prepositions to end sentences with.
—*William Safire*

## 2.21

I write for no other purpose than to add to the beauty that now belongs to me. I write a book for no other reason than to add three or four hundred acres to my magnificent estate. —*Jack London*

## 2.22

Harold Ross, when he was editor of The New Yorker, asked Ring Lardner just how he wrote his short stories. Lardner said he wrote a few widely separated words or phrases on a piece of paper and then went back and filled in the spaces. —*James Thurber*

## 2.23

Science fiction is something of an equal opportunity employer genre accommodating the likes of monsters, robots, aliens, creatures, clones, beasts, mutants, extraterrestrial phenomena, any combination of the above, and humans. —*Joanne Bernardi*

## 2.24

Whatever road I take, the guiding star is within me; the guiding star and the loadstone which point the way. They point in but one direction. They point to me. —*Ayn Rand*

## 2.25

Art is the desire of a man to express himself, to record the reactions of his personality to the world he lives in. —*Amy Lowell*

## 2.26

Every compulsion is put upon writers to become safe, polite, obedient, and sterile. In protest, I declined election to the National Institute of Arts and Letters some years ago, and now I must decline the Pulitzer Prize.

*—Sinclair Lewis*

## 2.27

Fiction is like a spider's web, attached ever so lightly perhaps, but still attached to life at all four corners. Often the attachment is scarcely perceptible. *—Virginia Woolf*

## 2.28

I've put in so many enigmas and puzzles that it will keep the professors busy for centuries arguing over what I meant, and that's the only way of insuring one's immortality. *—James Joyce*

## 2.29

A classic is something that everybody wants to have read and nobody wants to read. *—Mark Twain*

## 2.30

I would especially like to recourt the Muse of poetry, who ran off with the mailman four years ago, and drops me only a scribbled postcard from time to time. *—John Updike*

# ·· CHAPTER THREE: BUSINESS ··

## 3.1

He that is of the opinion money will do everything may well be suspected of doing everything for money. —*Benjamin Franklin*

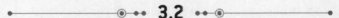

## 3.2

Even in such technical lines as engineering, about fifteen percent of one's financial success is due to one's technical knowledge and about eighty five percent is due to skill in human engineering, to personality and the ability to lead people. —*Dale Carnegie*

## 3.3

The fundamental principles which govern the handling of postage stamps and of millions of dollars are exactly the same. They are the common law of business, and the whole practice of commerce is founded on them.
—*P. D. Armour*

## 3.4

Business is like oil. It won't mix with anything but business. —*J. Graham*

## 3.5

The best executive is the one who has sense enough to pick good men to do what he wants done, and self-restraint to keep from meddling with them while they do it. —*Theodore Roosevelt*

## 3.6

I don't know the key to success, but the key to failure is trying to please everybody. —*Bill Cosby*

## 3.7

A business that makes nothing but money is a poor kind of business.
—*Henry Ford*

## 3.8

If eighty percent of your sales come from twenty percent of all your items, just carry those twenty percent. —*Henry Kissinger*

## 3.9

You do things when the opportunities come along. I've had periods in my life when I've had a bundle of ideas come along, and I've had long dry spells. If I get an idea next week, I'll do something. If not, I won't do a damn thing.
—*Warren Buffett*

## 3.10

Your most unhappy customers are your greatest source of learning.
—*Bill Gates*

## 3.11

The big corporations are suddenly taking notice of the web, and their reactions have been slow. Even the computer industry failed to see the importance of the Internet, but that's not saying much. Let's face it, the computer industry failed to see that the century would end.
—*Douglas Adams*

## 3.12

Concentrate your energies, your thoughts and your capital. The wise man puts all his eggs in one basket and watches the basket. —*Andrew Carnegie*

## 3.13

I don't think meals have any business being deductible. I'm for separation of calories and corporations. —*Ralph Nader*

## 3.14

Deals are my art form. Other people paint beautifully on canvas or write wonderful poetry. I like making deals, preferably big deals. —*Donald Trump*

## 3.15

And while the law of competition may be sometimes hard for the individual, it is best for the race, because it ensures the survival of the fittest in every department. —*Andrew Carnegie*

## 3.16

If the businessman would stop talking like a computer printout or a page from the corporate annual report, other people would stop thinking he had a cash register for a heart. —*Henry Kissinger*

## 3.17

Advertising may be described as the science of arresting the human intelligence long enough to get money from it. —*Stephen Butler Leacock*

## 3.18

Money has its limitations. While it may buy quantity, there is something beyond it and that is quality. —*Frank Lloyd Wright*

## 3.19

The most powerful pheromone known to science is the money pheromone. The corporate world is so suffused with it that almost anyone working in such an environment will be driven mad within a period of weeks. If you doubt this, you need only visit New York City and observe the effect of the proximity of Wall Street on a major urban population. —*David Gerrold*

## 3.20

The best way to prepare to be a programmer is to write programs and to study great programs that other people have written. In my case, I went to the garbage cans at the computer science center and I fished out listings of their operating system. —*Bill Gates*

## 3.21

Remember the waterfront shack with the sign, "Fresh Fish Sold Here?" Of course it's fresh: we're on the ocean. Of course it's for sale: we're not giving it away. Of course it's here, otherwise the sign would be someplace else. The final sign: "Fish." —*Noonan*

## 3.22

In many supermarkets, you'll find the beer right next to the diapers. Marketing analysts discovered that toward the end of the week diapers often are bought by men who have gotten calls to stop on the way home from work and pick up the weekend supply. So they pick up their weekend beer supply, too. —*Rochester Democrat and Chronicle*

## 3.23

The farmer is the only man in our economy who buys everything at retail, sells everything he sells at wholesale, and pays the freight both ways.
—*John F. Kennedy*

## 3.24

American business can outthink, outwork, outperform any nation in the world. But we can't beat the competition if we don't get in the ball game.
—*George Herbert Walker Bush*

## 3.25

I find it rather easy to portray a businessman. Being bland, rather cruel and incompetent comes naturally to me. —*John Cleese*

## 3.26

I had to make some optimistic assumptions to meet the revenue target. In week three, we're visited by an alien named D'utox Inag who offers to share his advanced technology. —*Dilbert*

## 3.27

If you want to increase your success rate, double your failure rate.
—*Thomas Watson*

## 3.28

Outstanding leaders go out of the way to boost the self-esteem of their personnel. If people believe in themselves, it's amazing what they can accomplish. —*Sam Walton*

## 3.29

It is unfortunate we can't buy many business executives for what they are worth and sell them for what they think they are worth. —*Malcolm Forbes*

## 3.30

It is well enough that people of the nation do not understand our banking and monetary system, for if they did, I believe there would be a revolution before tomorrow morning. —*Henry Ford*

## 3.31

The University of Illinois has hired fifteen women to smell pig manure all day so that researchers can find out what makes pig manure smell so bad. You know who I feel sorry for? The woman who applied for this job and got turned down. —*Jay Leno*

## 3.32

It is no secret that organized crime in America takes in over forty billion dollars a year. This is quite a profitable sum, especially when one considers that the Mafia spends very little for office supplies. —*Woody Allen*

# • • CHAPTER FOUR: ENTERTAINMENT • •

### 4.1

I stopped believing in Santa Claus when I was six. Mother took me to see him in a department store and he asked for my autograph. —*Shirley Temple*

### 4.2

To fulfill a dream, to be allowed to sweat over lonely labor, to be given a chance to create, is the meat and potatoes of life. The money is the gravy.
—*Bette Davis*

### 4.3

I don't want any yes-men around me. I want everyone to tell me the truth even if it costs him his job. —*Samuel Goldwyn*

### 4.4

Always remember that this whole thing was started by a mouse.
—*Walt Disney*

### 4.5

When the first publicity came out on The Twilight Zone, I was inundated by submissions from agents offering me six foot nine actors with long necks to which electrodes could easily be attached. —*Rod Serling*

### 4.6

God writes a lot of comedy. The trouble is, he's stuck with so many bad actors who don't know how to play funny. —*Garrison Keillor*

### 4.7

This film cost thirty one million dollars. With that kind of money I could have invaded some country. —*Clint Eastwood*

### 4.8

I'm not offended by all the dumb blonde jokes because I know I'm not dumb. And I also know that I'm not blonde. —*Dolly Parton*

## 4.9

In films murders are always very clean. I show how difficult it is and what a messy thing it is to kill a man. —*Alfred Hitchcock*

## 4.10

After the film was over someone suggested that maybe MGM should require an IQ test before allowing people into the theater. I can understand that point of view. If people do not have the courtesy to shut up during a film they should at least be segregated into special Saturday kiddie matinees no matter how advanced their years. —*Roger Ebert*

## 4.11

Animation can explain whatever the mind of man can conceive. This facility makes it the most versatile and explicit means of communication yet devised for quick mass appreciation. —*Walt Disney*

## 4.12

If you have made mistakes, there is always another chance for you. You may have a fresh start any moment you choose, for this thing we call failure is not the falling down but the staying down. —*Mary Pickford*

## 4.13

Television is the first truly democratic culture, the first culture available to everybody, and entirely governed by what the people want. The most terrifying thing is what people do want. —*Clive Barnes*

## 4.14

The only way he brushes his teeth is barefoot on the cold marble floor. He figures it is less work if he just holds the brush still and lets his teeth chatter. —*W.C. Fields*

## 4.15

It has been estimated that approximately fifty million people solve crossword puzzles. Consider it this way. The solvers would fill all the seats at Fenway Park in Boston for more than thirteen baseball seasons.
—*Eugene T. Maleska*

## 4.16

Meeting Alec Guinness at a Hollywood restaurant, James Dean insisted the older actor come outside and look at his new car. Alec glanced at the vehicle and said, "If you drive this car you won't be alive by next Thursday." Dean just laughed. Dean died on the road in that car less than a week later.
—*Liz Smith*

## 4.17

There are nitty gritty hazards during photography that drive film directors up a sound stage's padded walls. Time, for instance. A four million dollar budget and a two week shooting schedule mean a cost of over one hundred dollars per minute. Just a quick trip to the john will cost you over a thousand bucks. —*Bob Thomas*

## 4.18

I had learned that there's a huge difference between being in show business and being on top. It's the difference between turning a light on and sticking your finger in the light socket. —*Sonny Bono*

## 4.19

Children from the age of five to ten should watch more television. Television depicts adults as rotten SOBs given to fistfights, gunplay, and other mayhem. Kids who believe this about grownups aren't likely to argue about bedtime.
—*P.J. O'Rourke*

## 4.20

I never worry about main titles. I've seen clever ones which I've liked. But I think that clever main titles are a waste of money and a disservice to the film. The first shot of the film should be the most interesting thing the audience has seen since it sat down. —*Stanley Kubrick*

## 4.21

The last award of the evening went to Groucho Marx. Next to him on stage was a former Miss America who had also been named Miss Emmy. When he accepted, Groucho picked up Miss Emmy and carried her off, leaving his golden statuette behind him. —*Thomas O'Neil*

## 4.22

Philadelphia will always be dear to me because this was where I first tried that simple little prop that kept me alive all through my vaudeville days: track shoes. —*Bob Hope*

## 4.23

We are not trying to entertain the critics. I'll take my chances with the public. —*Walt Disney*

## 4.24

I find television very educating. Every time somebody turns on the set, I go into the other room and read a book. —*Groucho Marx*

## 4.25

The movies are the only business where you can go out front and applaud yourself. —*Will Rogers*

## 4.26

You know what your problem is, it's that you haven't seen enough movies. All of life's riddles are answered in the movies. —*Steve Martin*

## 4.27

Scientists are complaining that the new Dinosaur movie shows dinosaurs with lemurs, who didn't evolve for another million years. They're afraid the movie will give kids a mistaken impression. What about the fact that the dinosaurs are singing and dancing? —*Jay Leno*

## 4.28

I'm a foe of moderation, the champion of excess. If I may lift a line from a die-hard whose identity is lost in the shuffle, I'd rather be strongly wrong than weakly right. —*Tallulah Bankhead*

## 4.29

I hope we don't get to the point where we have to have the cat stop chasing the mouse to teach him glassblowing and basket weaving. —*Joseph Barbera*

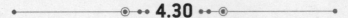

## 4.30

Most orgies that you go to, I have found, most of it is sad. All that wildness, all those laughs were like the shining silver and gold paper on packages, but there was nothing inside. —*Sammy Davis, Jr.*

## 4.31

If anybody says their facelift doesn't hurt, they're lying. It was like I'd spent the night with an axe murderer. —*Sharon Osbourne*

## 4.32

The animated cartoon is just about the purest, least arguable, most invigorating art form invented since mankind did shadow shows with wriggling fingers.
—*Ray Bradbury*

## 4.33

To give the Coyote a look of anticipatory delight, I draw everything up. The eyes are up, the ears are up, and even the nose is up. When he is defeated, on the other hand, everything turns down. —*Chuck Jones*

## 4.34

I want to have the fun of doing anime and I love anime, but I can't do storyboards because I can't really draw and that's what they live and die on.
—*Quentin Tarantino*

## 4.35

Radio is a medium of entertainment which permits millions of people to listen to the same joke at the same time, and yet remain lonesome.
—*T.S. Eliot*

## 4.36

I have no desire to prove anything by dancing. I have never used it as an outlet or a means of expressing myself. I just dance. I just put my feet in the air and move them around. —*Fred Astaire*

## 5.1

I do not like broccoli. And I haven't liked it since I was a little kid and my mother made me eat it. And I'm President of the United States and I'm not going to eat any more broccoli. —*George (H.W.) Bush*

## 5.2

Plain fare gives as much pleasure as a costly diet, while bread and water confer the highest possible pleasure when they are brought to hungry lips.
—*Epicurus*

## 5.3

I tell kids they should throw away the cereal and eat the box. At least they'd get some fiber. —*Richard Holstein*

## 5.4

Cold soup is a very tricky thing and it is the rare hostess who can carry it off. More often than not the dinner guest is left with the impression that had he only come a little earlier he could have gotten it while it was still hot.
—*Fran Lebowitz*

## 5.5

The best way to lose weight is to close your mouth, something very difficult for a politician. Or watch your food. Just watch it, don't eat it.
—*Edward Koch*

## 5.6

My doctor told me to stop having intimate dinners for four. Unless there are three other people. —*Orson Welles*

## 5.7

The only way to keep your health is to eat what you don't want, drink what you don't like, and do what you'd rather not. —*Mark Twain*

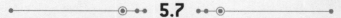

## 5.8

Half the cookbooks tell you how to cook the food, the other half tell you how to avoid eating it. —*Andy Rooney*

## 5.9

Thanksgiving dinners take eighteen hours to prepare. They are consumed in twelve minutes. Half-times take twelve minutes. This is not coincidence.
—*Erma Bombeck*

## 5.10

In order to know whether a human being is young or old, offer it food of different kinds at short intervals. If young, it will eat anything at any hour of the day or night. If old, it observes stated periods. —*Oliver Wendell Holmes*

## 5.11

Chowder breathes reassurance. It steams consolation.
—*Clementine Paddleford*

## 5.12

The public buys its opinions as it buys its meat or takes in its milk. On the principle that it is cheaper to do this than to keep a cow. So it is but the milk is more likely to be watered. —*Samuel Butler*

## 5.13

Don't take a butcher's advice on how to cook meat. If he knew, he'd be a chef.
—*Andy Rooney*

## 5.14

My mother was a good recreational cook, but what she basically believed about cooking was that if you worked hard and prospered, someone else would do it for you. —*Nora Ephron*

## 5.15

The highway is replete with culinary land mines disguised as quaint local restaurants that carry such reassuring names as Millie's, Pop's and Capt'n Dick's. —*Bryan Miller*

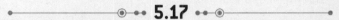

## 5.16

As for butter versus margarine, I trust cows more than chemists.
—*Joan Gussow*

## 5.17

Wine is a living liquid containing no preservatives. Its life cycle comprises youth, maturity, old age, and death. When not treated with reasonable respect it will sicken and die. —*Julia Child*

## 5.18

If penicillin can cure those that are ill, Spanish sherry can bring the dead back to life. —*Sir Alexander Fleming*

## 5.19

A cheese may disappoint. It may be dull, it may be naive, it may be oversophisticated. Yet it remains, cheese, milk's leap toward immortality.
—*Clifton Fadima*

# • • CHAPTER SIX: GREAT MINDS • •

## 6.1

Thinking is the hardest work there is. Which is the probable reason why so few engage in it. —*Henry Ford*

## 6.2

Just because something doesn't do what you planned it to do doesn't mean it's useless. —*Thomas Alva Edison*

## 6.3

Reading made Don Quixote a gentleman. Believing what he read made him mad. —*George Bernard Shaw*

## 6.4

Own only what you can carry with you; know language, know countries, know people. Let your memory be your travel bag. —*Alexander Solzhenitsyn*

## 6.5

I am an agnostic; I do not pretend to know what many ignorant men are sure of. —*Clarence Darrow*

## 6.6

Everybody gets so much information all day long that they lose their common sense. —*Gertrude Stein*

## 6.7

No one can be a great thinker who does not recognize that as a thinker it is his first duty to follow his intellect to whatever conclusions it may lead.
—*John Stuart Mill*

## 6.8

If you want to inspire confidence, give plenty of statistics. It does not matter that they should be accurate, or even intelligible, as long as there is enough of them. —*Lewis Carroll*

## 6.9

It is change, continuing change, inevitable change, that is the dominant factor in society today. This, in turn, means that our statesmen, our businessmen, our everyman must take on a science-fictional way of thinking. —*Isaac Asimov*

## 6.10

Don't tell people how to do things, tell them what to do and let them surprise you with their results. —*George S. Patton*

## 6.11

The things that will destroy us are: politics without principle; pleasure without conscience; wealth without work; knowledge without character; business without morality; science without humanity; and worship without sacrifice. —*Mahatma Gandhi*

## 6.12

Teaching was the hardest work I had ever done, and it remains the hardest work I have done to date. —*Ann Richards*

## 6.13

Don't be in a hurry to condemn because he doesn't do what you do or think as you think or as fast. There was a time when you didn't know what you know today. —*Malcolm X*

## 6.14

I know you've heard it a thousand times before. But it's true. Hard work pays off. If you want to be good, you have to practice, practice, practice. If you don't love something, then don't do it. —*Ray Bradbury*

## 6.15

Some minds seem almost to create themselves, springing up under every disadvantage and working their solitary but irresistible way through a thousand obstacles. —*Washington Irving*

## 6.16

Never doubt that a small group of thoughtful, committed citizens can change the world. Indeed, it's the only thing that ever has. —*Margaret Mead*

## 6.17

Keep away from people who try to belittle your ambitions. Small people always do that, but the really great make you feel that you, too, can become great. —*Mark Twain*

## 6.18

When I was a small boy growing up in Kansas, a friend of mine and I went fishing and as we sat there in the warmth of a summer afternoon on a riverbank we talked about what we wanted to do when we grew up. I told him that I wanted to be a real major-league baseball player, a genuine professional like Honus Wagner. My friend said that he'd like to be President of the United States. Neither of us got our wish. —*Dwight David Eisenhower*

## 6.19

Truth is like all beautiful things in the world; it does not disclose its desirability except to those who first feel the influence of falsehood.
—*Kahlil Gibran*

## 6.20

Anybody can become angry. That is easy; but to be angry with the right person, and to the right degree, and at the right time, and for the right purpose, and in the right way—that is not within everybody's power and is not easy. —*Aristotle*

## 6.21

Free speech is to a great people what winds are to oceans and malarial regions which waft away the elements of disease and bring new elements of health, and where free speech is stopped miasma is bred and death comes fast. —*Henry Ward Beecher*

## 6.22

I do not feel obliged to believe that the same God who endowed us with sense reason and intellect has intended us to forgo their use. —*Galileo Galilei*

## 6.23

It is the height of absurdity to sow little but weeds in the first half of one's lifetime and expect to harvest a valuable crop in the second half.
—*Percy Johnston*

## 6.24

The reasonable man adapts himself to the world. The unreasonable one persists in trying to adapt the world to himself. Therefore, all progress depends on the unreasonable man. —*George Bernard Shaw*

## 6.25

We have been godlike in our planned breeding of our domesticated plants and animals, but we have been rabbitlike in our unplanned breeding of ourselves. —*Arnold Joseph Toynbee*

## 6.26

If a man is called a streetsweeper, he should sweep streets, even as Michelangelo painted or Beethoven played music or Shakespeare wrote poetry. He should sweep streets so well that all the hosts of heaven and earth will pause to say here lived a great streetsweeper who did his job well.
—*Martin Luther King Jr.*

## 6.27

An education isn't how much you have committed to memory, or even how much you know. It's being able to differentiate between what you do know and what you don't. —*Anatole France*

## 6.28

I have known a vast quantity of nonsense talked about bad men not looking you in the face. Don't trust that conventional idea. Dishonesty will stare honesty out of countenance any day of the week if there is anything to be got by it. —*Charles Dickens*

## 6.29

There is no law, natural or divine, which demands that the world we live in become poorer, harsher, and more dangerous. If it continues to become that way, it is only because we do it to ourselves. —*Isaac Asimov*

## 6.30

Happiness consists more in small conveniences of pleasures that occur every day, than in great pieces of good fortune that happen but seldom to a man in the course of his life. —*Ben Franklin*

## 6.31

The degree of one's emotion varies inversely with one's knowledge of the facts. The less you know the hotter you get. —*Bertrand Russell*

## 6.32

Those who cannot remember the past are condemned to repeat it.
—*George Santayana*

## 6.33

Understanding can overcome any situation, however mysterious or insurmountable it may appear to be. —*Norman Vincent Peale*

## 6.34

I hope I shall always possess firmness and virtue enough to maintain what I consider the most enviable of all titles, the character of an honest man.
—*George Washington*

## 6.35

History is the version of past events that people have decided to agree upon.
—*Napoleon Bonaparte*

## 6.36

God alone knows the future, but only an historian can alter the past.
—*Ambrose Bierce*

## 6.37

Man is the only creature that consumes without producing. He does not give milk, he does not lay eggs, he is too weak to pull the plough, he cannot run fast enough to catch rabbits. Yet he is lord of all the animals.
—*George Orwell*

## 6.38

As long as the world shall last there will be wrongs, and if no man objected and no man rebelled, those wrongs would last forever. —*Clarence Darrow*

## 6.39

Travel is fatal to prejudice, bigotry, and narrow-mindedness, and many of our people need it sorely on these accounts. Broad, wholesome, charitable views of men and things cannot be acquired by vegetating in one little corner of the earth all one's lifetime. —*Mark Twain*

## 6.40

I am mortified to be told that, in the United States of America, the sale of a book can become a subject of inquiry, and of criminal inquiry too.
—*Thomas Jefferson*

## 6.41

I am somehow less interested in the weight and convolutions of Einstein's brain than in the near certainty that people of equal talent have lived and died in cotton fields and sweatshops. —*Stephen Jay Gould*

# ·· *CHAPTER SEVEN: HUMOR* ··

## 7.1

The only rules comedy can tolerate are those of taste, and the only limitations those of libel. —*James Thurber*

## 7.2

The most remarkable thing about my mother is that for thirty years she served the family nothing but leftovers. The original meal has never been found. —*Calvin Trillin*

## 7.3

The statistics on sanity are that one out of every four Americans is suffering from some form of mental illness. Think of your three best friends. If they are okay, then it's you. —*Rita Mae Brown*

## 7.4

USA Today has come out with a new survey: Apparently three out of four people make up seventy-five percent of the population. —*David Letterman*

## 7.5

Organized crime in America takes in over forty billion dollars a year and spends very little on office supplies. —*Woody Allen*

## 7.6

There was a time when a fool and his money were soon parted, but now it happens to everybody. —*Adlai Stevenson*

## 7.7

The embarrassing thing is that the salad dressing is outgrossing my films.
—*Paul Newman*

## 7.8

It has always surprised me how little attention philosophers have paid to humor, since it is a more significant process of mind than reason. Reason can only sort out perceptions, but the humor process is involved in changing them. —*Edward de Bono*

## 7.9

If a person is not talented enough to be a novelist, not smart enough to be a lawyer, and his hands are too shaky to perform operations, he becomes a journalist. —*Norman Mailer*

## 7.10

The minute that you read something that you can't understand, you can almost be sure it was drawn up by a lawyer. —*Will Rogers*

## 7.11

My generation, faced as it grew with a choice between religious belief and existential despair, chose marijuana. Now we are in our Cabernet stage.
—*Peggy Noonan*

## 7.12

Let me tell you something that we Israelis have against Moses. He took us forty years through the desert in order to bring us to the one spot in the Middle East that has no oil. —*Golda Meir*

## 7.13

As I have discovered by examining my past, I started out as a child. Coincidentally so did my brother. My mother did not put all her eggs in one basket, so to speak. She gave me a younger brother named Russell who taught me what was meant by survival of the fittest. —*Bill Cosby*

## 7.14

The capacity of human beings to bore one another seems to be vastly greater than that of any other animal. —*H. L. Mencken*

## 7.15

Imagination is a quality given a man to compensate him for what he is not, and a sense of humor was provided to console him for what he is.
—*Oscar Wilde*

## 7.16

America is the country where you buy a lifetime supply of aspirin for one dollar and use it up in two weeks. —*John Barrymore*

## 7.17

It takes little talent to see what is under one's nose; a good deal of it to know in what direction to point that organ. —*W. H. Auden*

## 7.18

If you can't ignore an insult, top it. If you can't top it, laugh it off. And if you can't laugh it off, it's probably deserved. —*Russell Lynes*

## 7.19

Randolph Churchill went into the hospital to have a lung removed. It was announced that the trouble was not malignant. It was a typical triumph of modern science to find the only part of Randolph that was not malignant and remove it. —*Evelyn Waugh*

## 7.20

A missionary, seeing a shabby man below her second story window, put ten dollars in an envelope, wrote "don't despair" on it, and dropped it to the man. Answering her bell the next day, she was given a wad of bills by the same man. "Don't Despair came in five to one," he smiled. —*C.R. Swindol*

## 7.21

It is no accident that, almost without exception, the section of our anatomy most firmly packed is neither our head, which often contains the brain, nor our bosom, where languishes our heart. —*Walt Kelly*

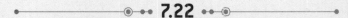

## 7.22

The best measure of a man's honesty isn't his income tax return. It's the zero adjust on his bathroom scale. —*Arthur C. Clarke*

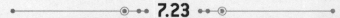

## 7.23

Whenever I see an old lady slip and fall on a wet sidewalk, my first instinct is to laugh. But then I think, what if I was an ant, and she fell on me. Then it wouldn't seem quite so funny. —*Jack Handey*

## 7.24

I know the answer! The answer lies within the heart of all mankind! The answer is twelve? I think I'm in the wrong building. —*Charles Schulz*

## 7.25

Parties who want milk should not seat themselves on a stool in the middle of the field in hopes that the cow will back up to them. —*Elbert Hubbard*

## 7.26

The odds of going to the store for a loaf of bread and coming out with only a loaf of bread are three billion to one. —*Erma Bombeck*

## 7.27

My whole life is waiting for the questions to which I have prepared answers.
—*Tom Stoppard*

## 7.28

I like Florida. Everything is in the eighties. The temperatures, the ages and the IQ's. —*George Carlin*

## 7.29

Not being able to sleep is terrible. You have the misery of having partied all night without the satisfaction. —*Lynn Johnston*

 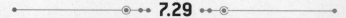

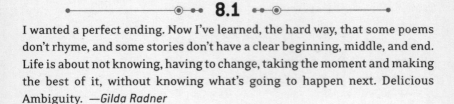

# • • *CHAPTER EIGHT: LIFE & DEATH* • •

## 8.1

I wanted a perfect ending. Now I've learned, the hard way, that some poems don't rhyme, and some stories don't have a clear beginning, middle, and end. Life is about not knowing, having to change, taking the moment and making the best of it, without knowing what's going to happen next. Delicious Ambiguity. —*Gilda Radner*

## 8.2

Dying is a very dull, dreary affair. And my advice to you is to have nothing whatever to do with it. —*W. Somerset Maugham*

## 8.3

I want to die in my sleep like my grandfather. Not screaming and yelling like the passengers in his car. —*Will Shriner*

## 8.4

The fear of death is the most unjustified of all fears, for there's no risk of accident for someone who's dead. —*Albert Einstein*

## 8.5

According to most studies, people's number one fear is public speaking. Number two is death. Death is number two. Does that sound right? This means to the average person, if you go to a funeral, you're better off in the casket than doing the eulogy. —*Jerry Seinfeld*

## 8.6

Saliva causes cancer, but only if swallowed in small amounts over a long period of time. —*George Carlin*

## 8.7

All say, How hard it is that we have to die, a strange complaint to come from the mouths of people who have had to live. —*Mark Twain*

## 8.8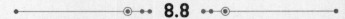

Because I could not stop for Death, He kindly stopped for me. The Carriage held but just ourselves. And Immortality  —*Emily Dickinson*

## 8.9

Years, following years, steal something every day; At last they steal us from ourselves away.  —*Horace*

## 8.10

When I die I shall be content to vanish into nothingness. No show, however good, could conceivably be good forever. I do not believe in immortality, and have no desire for it.  —*H.L. Mencken*

## 8.11

Thank Heaven the crisis, the danger, is past, and the lingering illness, is over at last, and the fever called Living is conquered at last.
                    —*Edgar Allan Poe*

## 8.12

Way I see it, we're all on the Hindenburg, no use fighting over the window seat.  —*Richard Jeni*

## 8.13

The good die young because they see it's no use living if you've got to be good.  —*John Barrymore*

## 8.14

When I look back on all these worries, I remember the story of the old man who said on his deathbed that he had had a lot of trouble in his life, most of which had never happened.  —*Sir Winston Churchill*

## 8.15

Life does not cease to be funny when people die any more than it ceases to be serious when people laugh.  —*George Bernard Shaw*

## 8.16

There's something about death that is comforting. The thought that you could die tomorrow frees you to appreciate life now. —*Angelina Jolie*

## 8.17

I do benefits for all religions. I'd hate to blow the hereafter on a technicality.
—*Bob Hope*

## 8.18

It's not true that life is one damn thing after another; it is one damn thing over and over. —*Edna St. Vincent Millay*

## 8.19

My formula for living is quite simple. I get up in the morning and I go to bed at night. In between, I occupy myself as best I can. —*Cary Grant*

## 8.20

It is possible to provide security against other ills, but as far as death is concerned, we men live in a city without walls. —*Epicurus*

## 8.21

Old age is ready to undertake tasks that youth shirked because they would take too long. —*William Somerset Maugham*

## 8.22

If people concentrated on the really important things in life, there'd be a shortage of fishing poles. —*Doug Larsen*

## 8.23

One-half the troubles of this life can be traced to saying yes too quickly and not saying no soon enough. —*Josh Billings*

## 8.24

To laugh often and much; to win the respect of intelligent people and the affection of children; to leave the world a better place; to know even one life has breathed easier because you have lived. This is to have succeeded.
—*Ralph Waldo Emerson*

## 8.25

Look, I really don't want to wax philosophic, but I will say that if you're alive, you've got to flap your arms and legs, you've got to jump around a lot, you've got to make a lot of noise, because life is the very opposite of death.
—*Mel Brooks*

## 8.26

Life's piano can only produce melodies of brotherhood and sisterhood when it is recognized that the black keys are as basic, necessary and beautiful as the white keys. —*Martin Luther King Jr.*

## 8.27

I have created a life by stepping out of the box of people's limitations. I call it zigging when others are zagging. It's a hoot. —*Oprah Winfrey*

## 8.28

The real sin against life is to abuse and destroy beauty, even one's own. Even more, one's own, for that has been put in our care and we are responsible for its well being. —*Katharine Anne Porter*

## 8.29

A life spent making mistakes is not only more honorable, but more useful than a life spent doing nothing. —*George Bernard Shaw*

## 8.30

Life must be lived forward, but it can only be understood backward.
—*Soren Kierkegaard*

## 8.31

Time is the coin of your life. It is the only coin you have, and only you can determine how it will be spent. Be careful lest you let other people spend it for you. —*Carl Sandburg*

## 8.32

Smoking is, if not my life, then at least my hobby. I love to smoke. Smoking is fun. Smoking is cool. Smoking is, as far as I am concerned, the entire point of being an adult. —*Fran Lebowitz*

## 8.33

Smoking kills. If you're killed, you've lost a very important part of your life.
—*Brooke Shields*

## 8.34

My life has no purpose, no direction, no aim, no meaning, and yet I'm happy. I can't figure it out. What am I doing right? —*Charles M. Schulz*

# • • CHAPTER NINE: MEN & WOMEN • •

## 9.1

To keep your marriage brimming, with love in the wedding cup, whenever you're wrong, admit it; whenever you're right, shut up. —*Ogden Nash*

## 9.2

True love comes quietly, without banners or flashing lights. If you hear bells, get your ears checked. —*Erich Segal*

## 9.3

I've yet to be on a campus where most women weren't worrying about some aspect of combining marriage, children, and a career. I've yet to find one where many men were worrying about the same thing. —*Gloria Steinem*

## 9.4

If a woman has to choose between catching a fly ball and saving an infant's life, she will choose to save the infant's life without even considering if there are men on base. —*Dave Barry*

## 9.5

Any man who can drive safely while kissing a pretty girl is simply not giving the kiss the attention it deserves. —*Albert Einstein*

## 9.6

Do you know what it means to come home at night to a woman who'll give you a little love, a little affection, a little tenderness? It means you're in the wrong house, that's what it means. —*Henny Youngman*

## 9.7

They say love is blind and marriage is an institution. Well, I'm not ready for an institution for the blind just yet. —*Mae West*

## 9.8

When marrying, ask yourself this question: Do you believe that you will be able to converse well with this person into your old age? Everything else in marriage is transitory. —*Friedrich Nietzsche*

## 9.9

Plain women know more about men than beautiful ones do, but beautiful women don't need to know about men. It's the men who have to know about beautiful women. —*Katharine Hepburn*

## 9.10

Being a woman is a terribly difficult task since it consists principally in dealing with men. —*Joseph Conrad*

## 9.11

Women speak because they wish to speak, whereas a man speaks only when driven to speech by something outside himself, like for instance he just can't find any clean socks. —*Jean Kerr*

## 9.12

A women's magazine once printed the replies of a number of famous women to the question, "what is the first thing you notice about a woman?" "Her way of speaking," was Agatha Christie's answer. "Her hands," said Maria Callas. "Her husband," replied Zsa Zsa. —*Clifton Fadiman*

## 9.13

Fifty three percent of women and fifty six percent of men opted for just OK sex in a clean house. But thirty one percent of women and thirty one percent of men wanted great sex in a dirty house. —*James Thornton*

## 9.14

When women are depressed, they either eat or go shopping. Men invade another country. It's a whole different way of thinking. —*Elaine Boosler*

## 9.15

Men forget everything; women remember everything. That's why men need instant replays in sports. They've already forgotten what happened.
—*Rita Rudner*

## 9.16

Lady Nancy Astor, Viscountess: "If you were my husband, Winston, I should flavour your coffee with poison." Winston Churchill: "If I were your husband, madam, I should drink it."

## 9.17

A man can be short and dumpy and getting bald but if he has fire, women will like him. —*Mae West*

## 9.18

Sometimes I wonder if men and women really suit each other. Perhaps they should live next door and just visit now and then. —*Katharine Hepburn*

## 9.19

They say women talk too much. If you have worked in Congress you know that the filibuster was invented by men. —*Clare Booth Luce*

## 9.20

Fighting is essentially a masculine idea; a woman's weapon is her tongue.
—*Hermione Gingold*

## 9.21

There we were in the middle of a sexual revolution wearing clothes that guaranteed we wouldn't get laid. —*Denis Leary*

## 9.22

Dancing is wonderful training for girls; it's the first way you learn to guess what a man is going to do before he does it. —*Christopher Morley*

## 9.23

I blame my mother for my poor sex life. All she told me was "the man goes on top and the woman underneath." For three years my husband and I slept in bunk beds. —*Joan Rivers*

# •• CHAPTER TEN: MUSIC ••

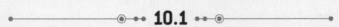

**10.1**

The memory of things gone is important to a jazz musician. Things like old folks singing in the moonlight in the back yard on a hot night or something said long ago. —*Louis Armstrong*

**10.2**

Roaming through the jungle of oohs and ahs, searching for a more agreeable noise, I live a life of primitivity with the mind of a child and an unquenchable thirst for sharps and flats. —*Duke Ellington*

**10.3**

I was born with music inside me. Music was one of my parts. Like my ribs, my kidneys, my liver, my heart. Like my blood. It was a force already within me when I arrived on the scene. It was a necessity for me like food or water.
—*Ray Charles*

**10.4**

My version of Georgia became the state song of Georgia. That was a big thing for me, man. It really touched me. Here is a state that used to lynch people like me suddenly declaring my version of a song as its state song. That is touching. —*Ray Charles*

**10.5**

I don't know anything about music. In my line you don't have to.
—*Elvis Presley*

**10.6**

The Mandolin is the bottom four strings of the guitar, backwards so a person with dyslexia has no problem learning to play the Mandolin.
—*Steve Goodman*

## 10.7

I understand the inventor of the bagpipes was inspired when he saw a man carrying an indignant, asthmatic pig under his arm. Unfortunately, the man made sound never equaled the purity of the sound achieved by the pig.
—*Alfred Hitchcock*

## 10.8

Rock gives children, on a silver platter, with all the public authority of the entertainment industry, everything their parents always used to tell them they had to wait for until they grew up and would understand later.
—*Allan Bloom*

## 10.9

A painter paints pictures on canvas. But musicians paint their pictures on silence. —*Leopold Stokowski*

## 10.10

If a composer could say what he had to say in words he would not bother trying to say it in music. —*Gustav Mahler*

## 10.11

The relation between practical and spiritual spheres in music is obvious, if only because it demands ears, finger, consciousness and intellect.
—*Luciano Berio*

## 10.12

I have never acknowledged the difference between serious music and light music. There is only good music and bad music. —*Kurt Weill*

## 10.13

The sonatas of Mozart are unique; they are too easy for children, and too difficult for artists. —*Arthur Schnabel*

## 10.14

After silence that which comes nearest to expressing the inexpressible is music. —*Aldous Huxley*

## 10.15

Take a music bath once or twice a week for a few seasons, and you will find that it is to the soul what the water-bath is to the body.
—*Oliver Wendell Holmes*

## 10.16

I have no pleasure in any man who despises music. It is no invention of ours: it is a gift of God. I place it next to theology. Satan hates music: he knows how it drives the evil spirit out of us. —*Martin Luther*

## 10.17

Everywhere in the world, music enhances a hall, with one exception: Carnegie Hall enhances the music. —*Isaac Stern*

## 10.18

If a man does not keep pace with his companions, perhaps it is because he hears a different drummer. Let him step to the music which he hears, however measured or far away. —*Henry David Thoreau*

## 10.19

Giuseppe Verdi's Maltese spaniel Lulu accompanied the composer everywhere concealed under his coat and served as a sounding board for his new compositions. —*Jon Winokur*

## 10.20

I have learned throughout my life as a composer chiefly through my mistakes and pursuits of false assumptions, not by my exposure to founts of wisdom and knowledge. —*Igor Stravinsky*

## 10.21

I could probably be an excellent lawyer, but I have no interest in that. Man, all my life I've never wanted to do anything but music. I can do other things. I can type sixty words a minute, but I don't plan on being a secretary.
—*Ray Charles*

**10.22**

The calm of our neighborhood is sometimes shattered by five boys in a nearby house practicing their rock band. One day their house was burgled. Seeing the police outside, a neighbor rushed over and asked "did they get the drums?" —*Diane Carswell*

**10.23**

Learning to read music in Braille and play by ear helped me develop a damn good memory. —*Ray Charles*

**10.24**

Jazz went from the classics to ragtime to Dixieland to swing to bebop to cool jazz. But it's always jazz. You can put a new dress on her, a new hat, but no matter what kind of clothes you put on her, she's the same old broad.
—*Lionel Hampton*

**10.25**

Music is your own experience, your own thoughts, your wisdom. If you don't live it, it won't come out of your horn. They teach you there's a boundary line to music. But, man, there's no boundary line to art. —*Charlie Parker*

# • • CHAPTER ELEVEN: POLITICS • •

## 11.1

When I was a boy I was told that anybody could become President. Now I'm beginning to believe it. —*Clarence Darrow*

## 11.2

One must change one's tactics every ten years if one wishes to maintain one's superiority. —*Napoleon Bonaparte*

## 11.3

In the short run, the market is a voting machine but in the long run it is a weighing machine. —*Warren Buffett*

## 11.4

I tried to walk a line between acting lawfully and testifying falsely, but I now realize that I did not fully accomplish that goal. —*Bill Clinton*

## 11.5

Squeezing our money out of politicians is more difficult than squeezing blood from a turnip. To paraphrase an Oscar Hammerstein love song, once they have found a way to take our money, they never let it go. —*Cal Thomas*

## 11.6

Let us not seek the Republican answer or the Democratic answer but the right answer. —*John F. Kennedy*

## 11.7

Mothers all want their sons to grow up to be president, but they don't want them to become politicians in the process. —*John F. Kennedy*

## 11.8

The White House: I don't know whether it's the finest public housing in America or the crown jewel of the prison system. —*Bill Clinton*

One thing I have learned about the presidency is that whatever shortcomings you have, people are going to notice them and whatever strengths you have, you're going to need them. —*George W. Bush*

Political language is designed to make lies sound truthful and murder respectable, and to give an appearance of solidity to pure wind.
—*George Orwell*

Politics are almost as exciting as war and quite as dangerous. In war you can only be killed once, but in politics, many times. —*Winston Churchill*

Keeping books on social aid is capitalistic nonsense. I just use the money for the poor. I can't stop to count it. —*Evita Peron*

I couldn't help but say to Mr. Gorbachev just think how easy his task and mine might be in these meetings that we held if suddenly there was a threat to this world from another planet. We'd find out once and for all that we really are all human beings here on this earth together. —*Ronald Reagan*

The only difference between the Republican and Democratic parties is the velocities with which their knees hit the floor when corporations knock on their door. That's the only difference. —*Ralph Nader*

Government's role should be only to keep the playing field level, and to work hand in hand with business on issues such as employment. But beyond this, to as great an extent as possible, it should get the hell out of the way.
—*Jesse Ventura*

## 11.16

I hope I shall possess firmness and virtue enough to maintain what I consider the most enviable of all titles, the character of an honest man.
—*George Washington*

## 11.17

I can think of nothing more boring for the American people than to have to sit in their living rooms for a whole half hour looking at my face on their television screens. —*Dwight D. Eisenhower*

## 11.18

The man who has never gone to school may steal from a freight car; but if he has a university education, he may steal the whole railroad.
—*Theodore Roosevelt*

## 11.19

Once a government is committed to the principle of silencing the voice of opposition, it has only one way to go, and that is down the path of increasingly repressive measures, until it becomes a source of terror to all its citizens and creates a country where everyone lives in fear. —*Harry S Truman*

## 11.20

To exclude from positions of trust and command all those below the age of forty four would have kept Jefferson from writing the Declaration of Independence, Washington from commanding the Continental Army, Madison from fathering the Constitution, Hamilton from serving as secretary of the treasury, Clay from being elected speaker of the House and Christopher Columbus from discovering America.
—*John Fitzgerald Kennedy*

## 11.21

The Clinton administration launched an attack on people in Texas because those people were religious nuts with guns. Hell, this country was founded by religious nuts with guns. Who does Bill Clinton think stepped ashore on Plymouth Rock? —*P.J. O'Roarke*

## 11.22

You can't be a real country unless you have a beer and an airline. It helps if you have some kind of a football team, or some nuclear weapons, but at the very least you need a beer. —*Frank Zappa*

## 11.23

The American wage earner and the American housewife are a lot better economists than most economists care to admit. They know that a government big enough to give you everything you want is a government big enough to take from you everything you have. —*Gerald R. Ford*

## 11.24

A journalist is a grumbler, a censurer, a giver of advice, a regent of sovereigns, a tutor of nations. Four hostile newspapers are more to be feared than a thousand bayonets. —*Napoleon Bonaparte*

## 11.25

Those who would give up essential liberty to purchase a little temporary safety deserve neither liberty nor safety. —*Benjamin Franklin*

## 11.26

All propaganda has to be popular and has to adapt its spiritual level to the perception of the least intelligent of those towards whom it intends to direct itself. —*Adolf Hitler*

## 11.27

The inherent vice of capitalism is the unequal sharing of blessings. The inherent virtue of socialism is the equal sharing of miseries.
—*Winston Churchill*

## 11.28

Ninety eight percent of the adults in this country are decent hardworking honest Americans. It's the other lousy two percent that get all the publicity, but then we elected them. —*Lily Tomlin*

### 11.29

Being president is like being a jackass in a hailstorm. There's nothing to do but stand there and take it. —*Lyndon Baines Johnson*

### 11.30

A gentleman haranguing on the protection of our law, and that it was equally open to the poor and the rich, was answered by another, "so is the London tavern." —*Tom Paine's Jests*

### 11.31

Some experts and Harry Truman said Abigail Adams would have made a better president than her husband. But I don't know. She had a lot more charm and tact, but she was a flaming radical, and wanted to free the slaves, educate children, and tax whiskey. She even mentioned votes for women.
—*Barbara Holland*

### 11.32

I'm not a palm pilot person. I'm an old fashioned write it down and remember it person. I have a palm pilot and, you know what, if I don't have my reading glasses, I can't read it. —*Hillary Rodham Clinton*

### 11.33

The Supreme Court has ruled that they cannot have a nativity scene in Washington, D.C. This wasn't for any religious reasons. They couldn't find three wise men and a virgin. —*Jay Leno*

### 11.34

If pigs could vote, the man with the slop bucket would be elected swineherd every time, no matter how much slaughtering he did on the side.
—*Orson Scott Card*

## 11.35

Everybody is in favor of free speech. Hardly a day passes without its being extolled, but some people's idea of it is that they are free to say what they like, but if anyone says anything back, that is an outrage. —*Winston Churchill*

## 11.36

If you are neutral in situations of injustice, you have chosen the side of the oppressor. If an elephant has its foot on the tail of a mouse and you say that you are neutral, the mouse will not appreciate your neutrality.
—*Bishop Desmond Tutu*

## 11.37

Tax reform means "Don't tax you, don't tax me, tax that fellow behind the tree." —*Russell B. Long*

## 11.38

There are not enough jails, not enough policemen, not enough courts to enforce a law not supported by the people. —*Hubert H. Humphrey*

## 11.39

No diet will remove all the fat from your body because the brain is entirely fat. Without a brain, you might look good, but all you could do is run for public office. —*George Bernard Shaw*

## 11.40

Never do anything against conscience even if the state demands it.
—*Albert Einstein*

## 11.41

True terror is to wake up one morning and discover that your high school class is running the country. —*Kurt Vonnegut*

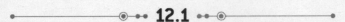

# •• *CHAPTER TWELVE: SCIENCE* ••

### 12.1

Computers make it easier to do a lot of things, but most of the things they make it easier to do don't need to be done. —*Andy Rooney*

### 12.2

The scientific theory I like best is that the rings of Saturn are composed entirely of lost airline luggage. —*Ernest Rutherford*

### 12.3

Never trust a computer you can't throw out a window. —*Steve Wozniak*

### 12.4

The best computer is a man, and it's the only one that can be mass produced by unskilled labor. —*Albert Einstein*

### 12.5

The saddest aspect of life right now is that science gathers knowledge faster than society gathers wisdom. —*Isaac Asimov*

### 12.6

We live in a society exquisitely dependent on science and technology, in which hardly anyone knows anything about science and technology.
—*Carl Sagan*

### 12.7

One day soon the Gillette company will announce the development of a razor that, thanks to a computer microchip, can actually travel ahead in time and shave beard hairs that don't even exist yet —*Dave Barry*

### 12.8

The future masters of technology will have to be light-hearted and intelligent. The machine easily masters the grim and the dumb. —*Marshall McLuhan*

## 12.9

I just invent, then wait until man comes around to needing what I've invented.
—*R. Buckminster Fuller*

## 12.10

The cloning of humans is on most of the lists of things to worry about from Science, along with behaviour control, genetic engineering, transplanted heads, computer poetry and the unrestrained growth of plastic flowers.
—*Lewis Thomas*

## 12.11

Medicine makes people ill, mathematics makes them sad, theology makes them sinful. —*Martin Luther*

## 12.12

Equipped with his five senses, man explores the universe around him and calls the adventure Science. —*Edwin Powell Hubble*

## 12.13

A fact is a simple statement that everyone believes. It is innocent, unless found guilty. A hypothesis is a novel suggestion that no one wants to believe. It is guilty, until found effective. —*Edward Teller*

## 12.14

Science is built up of facts, as a house is built of stones; but an accumulation of facts is no more a science than a heap of stones is a house.
—*Henri Poincare*

## 12.15

A science is any discipline in which the fool of this generation can go beyond the point reached by the genius of the last generation. —*Max Gluckman*

## 12.16

The scientist is not a person who gives the right answers, he's one who asks the right questions. —*Claude Levi-Strauss*

## 12.17

Physics is mathematical not because we know so much about the physical world, but because we know so little; it is only its mathematical properties that we can discover.  —*Bertrand Russell*

## 12.18

The quantum is that embarrassing little piece of thread that always hangs from the sweater of space-time. Pull it and the whole thing unravels.
—*Fred Alan Wolf*

## 12.19

If a man's wit be wandering, let him study the mathematics.  —*Francis Bacon*

## 12.20

All that glitters may not be gold, but at least it contains free electrons.
—*John Desmond Baernal*

## 12.21

We should take care not to make the intellect our god. It has, of course, powerful muscles, but no personality.  —*Albert Einstein*

## 12.22

There is one thing even more vital to science than intelligent methods; and that is, the sincere desire to find out the truth, whatever it may be.
—*Charles Sanders Pierce*

## 12.23

When NASA first started sending up astronauts, they quickly discovered that ballpoint pens would not work in zero gravity. To combat this problem, NASA scientists spent a decade and twelve billion dollars developing a pen that writes in zero gravity, upside down, under water, on almost any surface including glass and at temperatures ranging from below freezing to over three hundred centigrade. The Russians used a pencil.  —*Urban Legend*

## 12.24

The deepest sin against the human mind is to believe things without evidence. Science is simply common sense at its best. That is, rigidly accurate in observation, and merciless to fallacy in logic. —*Thomas Huxley*

## 12.25

When you are courting a nice girl an hour seems like a second. When you sit on a red hot cinder a second seems like an hour. That's relativity.
—*Albert Einstein*

## 12.26

The whole history of science has been the gradual realization that events do not happen in an arbitrary manner, but that they reflect a certain underlying order, which may or may not be divinely inspired. —*Stephen Hawking*

## 12.27

As societies grow decadent, the language grows decadent, too. Words are used to disguise, not to illuminate, action: you liberate a city by destroying it. Words are to confuse, so that at election time people will solemnly vote against their own interests. —*Gore Vidal*

## 12.28

We never stop investigating. We are never satisfied that we know enough to get by. Every question we answer leads on to another question. This has become the greatest survival trick of our species. —*Desmond Morris*

## 12.29

There is a theory which states that if ever anyone discovers exactly what the universe is for, and why it is here, it will instantly disappear and be replaced by something even more bizarre and inexplicable. There is another theory which states that this has already happened. —*Douglas Adams*

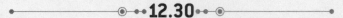

## 12.30

Interestingly, according to modern astronomers, space is finite. This is a very comforting thought, particularly for people who can never remember where they have left things. —*Woody Allen*

## 12.31

To me there is something superbly symbolic in the fact that an astronaut sent up as assistant to a series of computers found that he worked more accurately and more intelligently than they. —*Adlai E. Stevenson*

## 12.32

Give a person a fish and you feed them for a day; teach that person to use the Internet and they won't bother you for weeks. —*Anonymous*

## 12.33

There are companies actually working on giving your washing machine and toaster email addresses. Just wait until your home beef jerky smoker and other appliances start flooding your mailbox with goofy status messages.
—*Paul Somerson*

## 12.34

A new scientific truth does not triumph by convincing its opponents and making them see the light, but rather because its opponents eventually die, and a new generation grows up that is familiar with it. —*Max Planck*

## 12.35

Albert Einstein, who discovered that a tiny amount of mass is equal to a huge amount of energy, which explains why, as Einstein himself so eloquently put it in a famous speech to the Physics Department at Princeton, "You have to exercise for a week to work off the thigh fat from a single Snickers."
—*Dave Barry*

## 12.36

It is a mathematical fact that fifty percent of all doctors graduate in the bottom half of their class. —*Anon*

## 12.37

Technology frightens me to death. It's designed by engineers to impress other engineers, and they always come with instruction booklets that are written by engineers for other engineers, which is why almost no technology ever works. —*John Cleese*

## 12.38

It is of interest to note that while some dolphins are reported to have learned English, up to fifty words used in correct context, no human being has been reported to have learned dolphinese. —*Carl Sagan*

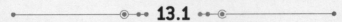

# • • CHAPTER THIRTEEN: SPORTS • •

## 13.1

It took me seventeen years to get three thousand hits in baseball. I did it in one afternoon on the golf course. —*Hank Aaron*

## 13.2

When you're playing against a stacked deck, compete even harder. Show the world how much you'll fight for the winners circle. If you do, someday the cellophane will crackle off a fresh pack, one that belongs to you, and the cards will be stacked in your favor. —*Pat Riley*

## 13.3

The spirit, the will to win, and the will to excel are the things that endure. These qualities are so much more important than the events that occur.
—*Vince Lombardi*

## 13.4

To me, boxing is like a ballet, except there's no music, no choreography and the dancers hit each other. —*Jack Handy*

## 13.5

Champions aren't made in the gyms. Champions are made from something they have deep inside them: A desire, a dream, a vision. —*Muhammad Ali*

## 13.6

I quit school in the sixth grade because of pneumonia. Not because I had it, but because I couldn't spell it. —*Rocky Graziano*

## 13.7

Losing streaks are funny. If you lose at the beginning, you get off to a bad start. If you lose in the middle of the season, you're in a slump. If you lose at the end, you're choking. —*Gene Mauch*

## 13.8

I always turn to the sports section first. The sports page records people's accomplishments; the front page has nothing but man's failures.

—*Earl Warren*

## 13.9

The difference between the old ballplayer and the new ballplayer is the jersey. The old ballplayer cared about the name on the front. The new ballplayer cares about the name on the back. —*Steve Garvey*

## 13.10

I don't believe professional athletes should be role models. I believe parents should be role models. It's not like it was when I was growing up. My mom and my grandmother told me how it was going to be. If I didn't like it, they said, Don't let the door hit you in the ass on your way out. Parents have to take better control. —*Charles Barkley*

## 13.11

When cerebral processes enter into sports, you start screwing up. It's like the Constitution, which says separate church and state. You have to separate mind and body. —*Bill Lee*

## 13.12

There is no room in your mind for negative thoughts. The busier you keep yourself with the particulars of shot assessment and execution, the less chance your mind has to dwell on the emotional. This is sheer intensity.

—*Jack Nicklaus*

## 13.13

Pro sports are a tough business. Whether you're in baseball, football, or something else. But when you're running around the bases after hitting a home run or jumping up and down after a touchdown, a little boy comes to the surface. —*Roy Campanella*

## 13.14

If you watch a game, it's fun. If you play it, it's recreation. If you work at it, it's golf. —*Bob Hope*

## 13.15

Baseball is almost the only orderly thing in a very unorderly world. If you get three strikes, even the best lawyer in the world can't get you off.
—*Bill Veeck*

## 13.16

If you are caught on a golf course during a storm and are afraid of lightning, hold up a one iron. Not even God can hit a one iron. —*Lee Trevino*

## 13.17

I figured that if I said it enough, I would convince the world that I really was the greatest. —*Muhammad Ali*

## 13.18

The wife of Akebono, the Hawaiian born sumo wrestler, gave birth recently to a seven pound seven ounce daughter. But Akebono wanted it made clear that he wears the diapers in the family. —*Rosenbloom, Chicago Tribune*

## 13.19

Of the dangers that confront an angler, the one seldom mentioned is the kitchen table. It is a repository of essential fishing tackle that never makes it to the fishing site. I laid a brand new flyrod on our kitchen table last summer and it was never seen again. —*Patrick McManus*

## 13.20

I'm not going to buy my kids an encyclopedia. Let them walk to school like I did. —*Yogi Berra*

## 13.21

All Americans believe that they are born fishermen. For a man to admit to a distaste for fishing would be like denouncing mother love and hating moonlight. —*John Steinbeck*

## 13.22

Fishing is much more than fish. It is the great occasion when we may return to the fine simplicity of our forefathers. —*Herbert Hoover*

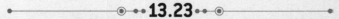

## 13.23

I've always swung the same way. The difference is when I swing and miss, people say, "He's swinging for the fences." But when I swing and make contact people say, "That's a nice swing." But there's no difference, it's the same swing. —*Sammy Sosa*

### 14.1

My factories may make an end of war sooner than your congresses. The day when two army corps can annihilate each other in one second, all civilized nations, it is to be hoped, will recoil from war and discharge their troops.

—*Alfred Nobel*

### 14.2

We stand today at a crossroads: One path leads to despair and utter hopelessness. The other leads to total extinction. Let us hope we have the wisdom to make the right choice. —*Woody Allen*

### 14.3

We often say how impressive power is but I do not find it impressive at all. The guns and the bombs, the rockets and the warships, are all symbols of human failure. They are necessary symbols, they protect what we cherish, but they are witness to human folly. —*Lyndon Baines Johnson*

### 14.4

The average bright young man who is drafted hates the whole business because an army always tries to eliminate the individual differences. in men. The theory is that a uniformity of action is necessary to achieve a common goal. That's good for an army but terrible for an individual who likes himself the way he is. —*Andrew A. Rooney (Andy Rooney)*

### 14.5

In perpetrating a revolution there are two requirements, someone or something to revolt against, and someone to actually show up and do the revolting. If either faction fails to attend, the whole enterprise is likely to come off badly. —*Woody Allen*

### 14.6

History teaches us that men and nations behave wisely once they have exhausted all other alternatives. —*Abba Eban*

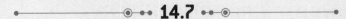

**14.7**

Diplomats are just as essential to starting a war as soldiers are for finishing it. You take diplomacy out of war and the thing would fall flat in a week.
—*Will Rogers*

**14.8**

A man who says that no patriot should attack the war until it is over is saying no good son should warn his mother of a cliff until she has fallen.
—*G.K. Chesterton*

**14.9**

The fact that the talk may be boring or turgid or uninspiring should not cause us to forget the fact that it is preferable to war.
—*Henry Cabot Lodge Jr.*

**14.10**

Man's greatest blunder has been in trying to make peace with the skies instead of making peace with his neighbors.  —*Elbert Hubbard*

**14.11**

I think that people want peace so much that one of these days government had better get out of their way and let them have it.  —*Dwight Eisenhower*

# CHAPTER FIFTEEN:
## •• WORDS OF WISDOM ••

### 15.1

The problem with people who have no vices is that generally you can be pretty sure they're going to have some pretty annoying virtues.
—*Elizabeth Taylor*

### 15.2

Rage is the only quality which has kept me, or anybody I have ever studied, writing columns for newspapers. —*Jimmy Breslin*

### 15.3

Too bad the only people who know how to run the country are busy driving cabs and cutting hair. —*George Burns*

### 15.4

I feel about airplanes the way I feel about diets. It seems to me they are wonderful things for other people to go on. —*Jean Kerr*

### 15.5

I pay no attention whatever to anybody's praise or blame. I simply follow my own feelings. —*Wolfgang Amadeus Mozart*

### 15.6

A man only learns in two ways, one by reading, and the other by association with smarter people. —*Will Rogers*

### 15.7

A King, realizing his incompetence, can either delegate or abdicate his duties. A Father can do neither. —*Marlene Dietrich*

### 15.8

Fashion is a form of ugliness so intolerable that we have to alter it every six months —*Oscar Wilde*

## 15.9

When lip service to some mysterious deity permits bestiality on Wednesday and absolution on Sunday, cash me out. —*Frank Sinatra*

## 15.10

You can safely assume that you've created God in your own image when it turns out that God hates all the same people you do. —*Anne Lamott*

## 15.11

Until you value yourself, you won't value your time. Until you value your time, you will not do anything with it. —*M. Scott Peck*

## 15.12

Lots of people want to ride with you in the limo, but what you want is someone who will take the bus with you when the limo breaks down.
—*Oprah Winfrey*

## 15.13

I expect to pass through this world but once. Any good therefore that I can do, or any kindness or abilities that I can show to any fellow creature, let me do it now. Let me not defer it or neglect it, for I shall not pass this way again.
—*William Penn*

## 15.14

Success is not the key to happiness. Happiness is the key to success. If you love what you are doing, you will be successful. —*Albert Schweitzer*

## 15.15

We spend all our time searching for security, and then we hate it when we get it. —*John Steinbeck*

## 15.16

Man is a special being and if left to himself in an isolated condition would be one of the weakest creatures but associated with his kind he works wonders. —*Daniel Webster*

## 15.17

Justice is a commodity which, in a more or less adulterated condition, the state sells to the citizen as a reward for his allegiance taxes and personal service. —*Ambrose Bierce*

## 15.18

People have to talk about something just to keep their voice boxes in working order so they'll have good voice boxes in case there's ever anything really meaningful to say. —*Kurt Vonnegut Jr.*

## 15.19

Language is the armory of the human mind and at once contains the trophies of its past and the weapons of its future conquests.
—*Samuel Taylor Coleridge*

## 15.20

Anyway, no drug, not even alcohol, causes the fundamental ills of society. If we're looking for the source of our troubles, we shouldn't test people for drugs. We should test them for stupidity, ignorance, greed, and love of power. —*P.J. O'Rourke*

## 15.21

No man can put a chain about the ankle of his fellow man without at last finding the other end fastened about his own neck. —*Frederick Douglass*

## 15.22

The metaphor of the melting pot is unfortunate and misleading. A more accurate analogy would be a salad bowl, for though the salad is an entity the lettuce can still be distinguished from the chicory, the tomatoes from the cabbage. —*Carl N. Degler*

## 15.23

Human beings who are almost unique in having the ability to learn from the experience of others are also remarkable for their apparent disinclination to do so. —*Douglas Adams*

**15.24**

The test of a first rate intelligence is the ability to hold two opposed ideas at the same time and still retain the ability to function. —*F. Scott Fitzgerald*

**15.25**

He presents me with what is always an acceptable gift who brings me news of a great thought before unknown. He enriches me without impoverishing himself. —*Ralph Waldo Emerson*

**15.26**

Don't think of retiring from the world until the world will be sorry that you retire. I hate a fellow whom pride or cowardice or laziness drive into a corner and who does nothing when he is there but sit and growl. Let him come out as I do and bark. —*Samuel Johnson*

**15.27**

To hold the same views at forty as we held at twenty is to have been stupefied for a score of years and take rank, not as a prophet, but as an unteachable brat well birched and none the wiser. —*Robert Louis Stevenson*

**15.28**

I have always been among those who believed that the greatest freedom of speech was the greatest safety, because if a man is a fool the best thing to do is to encourage him to advertise the fact by speaking. —*Woodrow Wilson*

**15.29**

Sometimes men come by the name of genius in the same way that certain insects come by the name of centipede, not because they have a hundred feet but because most people can't count above fourteen. —*G. C. Lichtenberg*

**15.30**

The more gross the fraud, the more glibly will it go down, and the more greedily be swallowed, since folly will always find faith where impostors will find imprudence. —*Charles Caleb Colton*

## 15.31

A man always has two reasons for what he does, a good one and the real one.
—*J.P. Morgan*

## 15.32

It's hard to argue against cynics. They always sound smarter than optimists because they have so much evidence on their side. —*Molly Ivins*

## 15.33

We do not have to visit a madhouse to find disordered minds. Our planet is the mental institution of the Universe. —*Johann Wolfgang von Goethe*

## 15.34

People often become actresses because of something they dislike about themselves: They pretend they are someone else. —*Bette Davis*

## 15.35

I've made an odd discovery. Every time I talk to a savant I feel quite sure that happiness is no longer a possibility. Yet when I talk with my gardener, I'm convinced of the opposite. —*Bertrand Russell*

## 15.36

All I can say is what I've always said: If you break your leg, stop thinking about dancing and start decorating the cast. —*Warren Zevon*

## 15.37

For a nation which has an almost evil reputation for bustle, bustle, bustle, and rush, rush, rush, we spend an enormous amount of time standing around in line in front of windows, just waiting. —*Robert Benchley*

## 15.38

If a man can write a better book, preach a better sermon, or make a better mousetrap, than his neighbor, though he build his house in the woods, the world will make a beaten path to his door. —*Ralph Waldo Emerson*

## 15.39

In a time of drastic change it is the learners who inherit the future. The learned usually find themselves equipped to live in a world that no longer exists. —*Eric Hoffer*

## 15.40

Hegel was right when he said that we learn from history that man can never learn anything from history. —*George Bernard Shaw*

## 15.41

Every past is worth condemning. —*Friedrich Nietzsche*

## 15.42

The first fall of snow is not only an event, it is a magical event. You go to bed in one kind of a world and wake up in another quite different, and if this is not enchantment then where is it to be found? —*J.B. Priestley*

## 15.43

Tell a man there are three hundred billion stars in the universe and he'll believe you. Tell him a bench has wet paint on it and he'll have to touch it to be sure. —*Albert Einstein*

## 15.44

If you judge people you have no time to love them. —*Mother Teresa*

## 15.45

Never tell people how to do things. Tell them what to do and they will surprise you with their ingenuity. —*George Smith Patton*

## 15.46

To be wronged is nothing unless you continue to remember it. —*Confucius*

## 15.47

Because we don't think about future generations, they will never forget us. —*Henrik Tikkanen*

## 15.48

The activist is not the man who says the river is dirty. The activist is the man who cleans up the river. *—Ross Perot*

## 15.49

Giving up doesn't always mean you are weak. Sometimes it means that you are strong enough to let go. *—Anon*

## 15.50

If you reject the food, ignore the customs, fear the religion and avoid the people, you might better stay home. *—James Michener*

### Easy Living

Summer is the season when the air pollution is much warmer.

### Note of Caution

Be careful about reading health books. You may die of a misprint.
*—Mark Twain*

### Senior Moment

Age carries all things away, even the mind. *—Virgil*

### Girl Crazy

Hell hath no fury like the lawyer of a woman scorned.

### Pigpen Cipher

Things will get better despite our efforts to improve them. *—Will Rogers*

### Bounceback Cipher

Anyone who has never made a mistake has never tried anything new.
*—Albert Einstein*

## Polybius Checkerboard

There's no such thing as fun for the whole family. —*Jerry Seinfeld*

## Column Code

If you look at the first letter in each row, going from top to bottom, it reads MEET ME AT TEN.

## Time Goes By

Middle age is when your age starts to show around your middle. —*Bob Hope*

## True Story

There are worse crimes than burning books. One of them is not reading them. —*Ray Bradbury*

## Telephone Code

I am not afraid of death. I just don't want to be there when it happens. —*Woody Allen*

## Cryptarithms

```
  8 3 2 0 7 9
+   6 5 4 3 8
= 8 9 7 5 1 7
```

## Our Town

London is a modern Babylon. —*Benjamin Disraeli*

## More Cryptarithms

```
   8972      A=6  B=5  C=7  D=8  E=2  I=9  L=1  O=3  S=4
+  3884
+   568

=13424
```

# Sticklinks

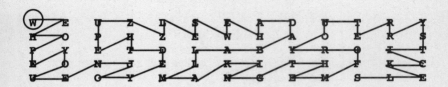

# ABOUT THE AUTHORS

**A**UTHOR and speaker **Terry Stickels** has dedicated his life to the pursuit of improving one's mental flexibility and creative problem solving skills . . . and making it fun. His books, calendars, card decks, and newspaper columns are filled with fun and challenging puzzles that stretch the minds of even the best thinkers.

Stickels is well known for his three internationally and nationally syndicated columns. *FRAME GAMES* and *STICKDOKU*, seen in *USA Weekend* magazine, are read by over 48,000,000 people in 600 newspapers weekly. He concurrently writes *STICKELERS*, a puzzle column syndicated daily by King Features, appearing in some of the largest newspapers in America, such as The *Washington Post*, *The Chicago-Sun Times*, and *The Seattle Post-Intelligencer*. You may have seen his puzzles on the back of Kellogg's Raisin Bran or on the Universal Studios website for the movie *A Beautiful Mind*, for which he created the most famous IQ quiz in Internet history. This was followed by three successful books requested by the high I.Q. society MENSA. In all, there are over 50 books, card decks, and calendars of puzzles ranging from geography to spatial/visual puzzles. You can see a list of Terry's work and other puzzle fun at www.terrystickels.com.

**Sam Bellotto Jr.** is a New York–based computer software developer and constructor of crossword puzzles. His company, Crossdown, makes and markets high-end word puzzle software and games. Bellotto contributes regularly to all of the major crossword puzzle markets including Simon & Schuster, *The New York Times,* and Random House. He also does a weekly crossword feature for a number of high-profile newspapers, such as *Back Stage, The Hill,* and *The Nantucket Independent*. For additional information about Sam or his word puzzle software, visit the Crossdown website at www.Crossdown.com.

A special mention goes to three important people responsible for bringing you this collection of Cryptograms. This book could never have been completed without their invaluable contributions and suggestions. Ms. Terry Baughan, Ms. Christy Davis, and Ms. Eleanor Joyner spent a great deal of time, effort, and intellectual firepower to assist Sam and Terry in bringing you the best book of puzzles they could deliver.

*Thank you.*